AUTHORITY *Abusers*

AUTHORITY Abusers

Toxic Leadership and Its Effects in Homes, Churches, and Relationships

WHITAKER
HOUSE

Publisher's Note:
Individuals' names and exact circumstances have been altered to protect privacy.

AUTHORITY ABUSERS

Toxic Leadership and Its Effects in Homes, Churches, and Relationships

George G. Bloomer
Bethel Family Worship Center
515 Dowd St.
Durham, NC 27701
www.bethelfamily.org

ISBN: 978-1-60374-046-3
Printed in the United States of America

Whitaker House
1030 Hunt Valley Circle
New Kensington, PA 15068
www.whitakerhouse.com

Library of Congress Cataloging-in-Publication Data
Bloomer, George G., 1963–
Authority abusers : toxic leadership and its effects in homes, churches, and relationships / G.G. Bloomer. —Rev. and expanded ed.
p. cm.
Summary: "Explains how to recognize abusive authority in homes, churches, and relationships, providing steps for deliverance and healing from the scars of abuse"—Provided by publisher.
ISBN 978-1-60374-046-3 (trade hardcover : alk. paper) 1. Christianity—Psychology. 2. Authority—Religious aspects—Christianity. I. Title.
BR110.B48 2008
262'.8—dc22 2008001414

1 2 3 4 5 6 7 8 9 10 11 12 W 16 15 14 13 12 11 10 09 08

CONTENTS

1

An Atmosphere of Abuse

And if anyone causes one of these little ones who believe in me to sin, it would be better for him to be thrown into the sea with a large millstone tied around his neck.
Mark 9:42 (NIV)

It is subtle and often invisible to those who are involved, but as deadly to the spirit as carbon monoxide is to the body. Police officers get jail time for it; parents lose custody of their children for it; but it happens every day in thousands of churches and families throughout the world.

I'm talking about authority abuse.

Most people have no idea how hurtful and destructive authority abuse can be. It's a complicated issue that is sometimes difficult to talk about. As with other forms of abuse, though, we must acknowledge that a problem exists before we can change for the better.

Exactly what is this problem? Is authority itself bad, something that should be avoided at all costs? Of course not. The problem is not with authority or even the use of authority. Rather, the problem is with people who abuse those under them and justify that abuse by their position of "authority." When this occurs, spirits are crushed and lives are broken.

Authority abuse is sin—a perversion of something beautiful. Such perversion can happen in any realm of life. For instance, sexual desire between a man and a woman is a beautiful thing in the context of marriage; that's how God designed it to be. Sex between a man and a prostitute, however, is an ugly, dirty thing that degrades both the man and woman involved because it does away with the holy intimacy God intended to be the focus of the marriage bed.

Godly authority is honest, loving, and liberating.

Similarly, godly authority is protective, loving, honest, and—above all—liberating, while the abuse of authority usually hinges on deception. Often, both the abuser and the abused are deceived, and such deception deprives people of God's love and the freedom of His truth.

Authority abuse stands between God and man, and it is thus a sin against the very body of Christ. By separating innocent, defenseless members from the head, which is Christ (see Colossians 1:18), authority abusers spiritually cripple those members; often, this crippling is permanent.

Only when we reject authority abuse can we embrace the authority God has designed to bless and prosper us. But that's getting ahead of the story.

A Parable

There were two brothers fresh out of college who began a start-up agricultural venture in the Midwest. One brother focused on farming, applying the latest technology and innovative strategies to produce several varieties of cattle feed. The other began breeding and raising cattle for beef, using state-of-the-art methods to track the herd's health and make breeding decisions. He bought feed exclusively from his brother, and the two developed a complex, highly personalized, but very profitable kickback plan for dividing their income.

By the time the brothers reached middle age, both were moderately wealthy, with the strongest young minds and bodies doing the daily managerial work for their agricultural estates. The summer that their combined worth topped four and a half million dollars, they turned off their cell phones and took their wives on a hunting vacation in the Rocky Mountains. They set no return date, only telling their foremen, "We'll be back when we both get our elk."

A month went by, and they were still gone. A month and two weeks. Two months. After two and a half months, the brothers returned with mountain tans, coolers full of hearty steaks, and one impressively mounted elk head apiece. The brother who raised beef found the office empty—one of his staff members was on a small, much-deserved family vacation,

> so the foreman was out on the range with the company helicopter, supervising the birth of twin calves. All the books were up-to-date; all the bills were current. Profits were slightly down, but everything was running smoothly and the foreman had logged more hours of work than any of the other help.
>
> The brother with the crop-producing business came home to a party in his honor—or, rather, a party in honor of the "summerlong vacation" the foreman figured his boss must be on. This was one of a series of drunken bashes the foreman had hosted; workers were required to help entertain his friends (he called them "business contacts") with no overtime pay. The office was full of empty coffee cups and doughnut boxes left over from the days the foreman spent there while everyone else was in the field.
>
> Profits were higher than ever before—at least they would have been, had it not been for the expensive parties. No one had been given vacation time, and no employee bonuses had been issued for two and a half months.
>
> Needless to say, the first foreman received a respectable bonus and a few extra days of paid vacation for his dedication and honest management. The second foreman was served a summary pink slip and couldn't even talk his way into a job pitching hay bales on and off the trucks.

You're probably not wondering why the second guy got fired. Nobody would protest, "But he made more money for the company!" It's more likely that you feel he got off easy because a person in his position is responsible for the well-being of other employees and should not spend company resources on his own recreation.

This man's behavior not only hurt the people he was supposed to motivate, encourage, and provide for, but it also undermined the goals he was driving them toward. (See Matthew 24:44–51.) This is a prime example of authority abuse in action.

Feed My Sheep

In John 21, Jesus told Peter how the church is to demonstrate Christ's love to His people:

> *When they had finished eating, Jesus said to Simon Peter, "Simon son of John, do you truly love me more than these?" "Yes, Lord," he said, "you know that I love you." Jesus said, "Feed my lambs." Again Jesus said, "Simon son of John, do you truly love me?" He answered, "Yes, Lord, you know that I love you." Jesus said, "Take care of my sheep." The third time he said to him, "Simon son of John, do you love me?" Peter was hurt because Jesus asked him the third time, "Do you love me?" He said, "Lord, you know all things; you know that I love you." Jesus said, "Feed my sheep."* (John 21:15–17 NIV)

Jesus' message to Peter is clear: loving Him means caring for (*"feeding"*) His little ones (*"lambs"*).

On the surface, the church seems to have remembered this. The manicured lawns, smiling faces, and open arms of greeters at church doors could be an inviting alternative to the rugged way of life offered in a society of corporate cataclysms and a "survival of the fittest" mentality. People are looking for acceptance, stability, and even guidance—ultimately, they're looking for God—and the church should be the end of this search.

> The church should be the end of the search for God.

Unfortunately, the glitzy showmanship and manipulative teaching of men who seek self-glorification rather than to reveal the glory of God often obstruct the acceptance, stability, guidance, and love that people seek. Thousands of people avoid Christians and refuse to attend church because the only message they have ever heard is one of judgment, criticism, and performance-based love.

Irresponsible leaders have made God's business—with its saving, grace-filled mission statement—infamous. They have turned the church into a place of rigid rules and stiff membership requirements, consequently turning seekers away from the God who can fulfill them.

In my twenty-three years of preaching, I have seen the following played out hundreds of times: a girl rebels against her parents, and, for a time, nothing they do works to bring her under control. She winds up getting pregnant.

Naturally, this jolts her to her senses; she returns to obeying her parents' rules and seeks to give her life back to God in repentance. It's a painful lesson, but at least she has learned it. She starts on her way to healing and renewal.

Then, authority figures at her local church intervene. They declare her to be an example of "sin in the camp" and demand that she leave her family and the church. Her mother is exiled from the choir, and her father is forced to step down as a deacon, all because their family is "tainted with sin."

I have to ask, "Where, in all of this, is the grace and forgiveness of Jesus Christ?" The answer is, "Nowhere." This is simply spiritual abuse and condemnation posing as godly authority; this is man enforcing rules that Christ never engineered. Time and again, I have seen lives devastated by this kind of abuse until I simply have to cry, "Enough!"

A few years ago, there were some serious scandals in the leadership of the United States Navy. Several high-ranking officials betrayed the trust given to them, mishandling both the resources and people put under their care.

The offenses were committed by only a handful of officers, while hundreds of loyal, honest men and women did their best to lead a strong and honorable branch of the armed services.

Authority abuse has corrupted the church in America.

Inevitably, though, people began associating the US Navy with corruption. The abuse of authority is a serious, deadly thing, and the breach in trust outweighed generations of unbroken integrity and courage.

The same thing has happened in the American church, but we can't blame it on one or two famous televangelists like the Navy could point fingers at just a few officers.

From small country parishes to metropolitan megachurches, it's possible to find pastors who abuse their position. The controlling, graceless dictatorship of man-centered religion knows no race or creed, gender or geography.

As a result, many stable Christian institutions, founded upon and continually following the Word of God, have been lumped together with the hypocritical, life-damaging minority. The Good News of Jesus Christ is continually hindered by self-proclaimed dictators in the guise of spiritual shepherds who actually lead the sheep astray.

Dictators disguised as spiritual shepherds hinder the Gospel.

A gentleman once told me that his church had a total of 147 people at every service, including Communion, baptismal services, and baby dedications. For years, there were never more than 147 people, and never fewer. Always exactly 147.

I asked him what kind of church it was, and the ministry he described sounded fairly decent. He explained, though, that the people of the church were absolutely terrified of the pastor and his wife. Apparently, the pastor and the first lady of the church had a say in the day-to-day lives of every member—daily duties, the way families were run, household finances—everything.

His story reminded me of my own experience growing up in church. As a young boy, I often prayed about my sins, but I did not worry about what God thought of them or of me!

My prayer was this: "Dear God, please don't let the pastor find out that I sinned." Because the pastor led a very dogmatic and legalistic church, I feared him more than I feared God. I was terrified that God might allow this man to know my thoughts and feelings without my even sharing them.

Situations like mine still exist. Even today, congregations suffocate in the poisonous atmosphere of an abusive authority. Many people have experienced a leader trying to control them by citing so-called "biblical obedience."

Too often (even once is too often!), a person submits himself to the abusive pastor or ministry leadership only to find out that he is being made a slave to the personal whims and erroneous convictions of that authority.

This control often goes so far as to dictate when families should go on vacations, how long couples should wait to consummate their marriage, where a family's children should attend school...sadly, the list goes on.

Countless people have been hurt by the institution originally established to bring them healing. Thus, there are many who truly and wholeheartedly love God but have no regard for the organized church.

There are many who love God but not the church.

Denominationalism, tradition, and authority abuse have left an unpleasant aftertaste in the mouths of congregation members who trusted and depended on their leaders.

Many pastors and leaders have become taskmasters in the lives of God's people instead of being leaders who offer accountability and care!

Authority Abuse Is a Device of Satan

Satan's desire has always been to exalt his position above the throne of God. He seeks to turn the world against the church and the God who upholds it, and he will use any willing vessel to achieve these goals.

Though the number of good pastors and good churches outnumber the horror story-inspiring, congregation-controlling dictators disguised as spiritual leaders, the enemy would like to magnify the few bad seeds to corrupt the entire institution as we know it.

How many people do you know who have totally turned their backs on the church and vowed never again to set foot in another Christian institution again because they have been hurt? Even though many people use this as an excuse not to come to church, we cannot ignore those who have sincerely been badgered, mishandled, and wounded by ungodly ministry.

It is now time for those of us in the body of Christ to break away from the man-made traditions and manipulative tactics of control that produce such wounds. But how can we prepare the road to recovery for those who've been injured, while simultaneously opening the eyes of others so they can avoid the same traps?

After my childhood pastor died, years after I had grown up and begun my own ministry, God began revealing to me just how deep was the darkness that had surrounded my former pastor's church.

God took me through a season of mental and spiritual purging during which my eyes were opened so that I would not unconsciously incorporate those same ungodly tactics into my own ministry.

In short, God began removing the mental barriers—barriers I put up in response to this abusive authority—that were preventing me from knowing God as He really is.

The more I understood about what true spiritual authority should look like and how this pastor had deviated from that truth, the more I understood God's character.

Now I know that it is only when we reject authority abuse that we can embrace the authority God has designed to bless and prosper us.

2

Godly Authority

God blessed them and said to them, "Be fruitful and increase in number; fill the earth and subdue it. Rule over the fish of the sea and the birds of the air and over every living creature that moves on the ground."
Genesis 1:28 (NIV)

The first house my wife Jeannie and I built was in a mostly undeveloped area with few houses nearby. After the land had been cleared and all the testing done, we formulated a site plan and thought we were well on our way to building an honest-to-goodness house.

To our amazement, though, we were soon billed $50,000 to lay the foundation and connect sewage and water pipes to the city of Durham! This meant $50,000 of our money was going into the ground before any piece of the house's structure was visible.

Eventually the house was built, and we furnished it and moved in. As years passed, though, the foundation and house began settling, and problems with the house's underground mechanics began to surface. Before it was all over, we had to dig four feet below ground to fix the faulty foundation.

Matthew 7:24 reminds us that whoever hears Christ's teachings and puts them into practice is like a wise man who builds his house upon a rock or a solid foundation. The person who builds on the Word of God is well-equipped to withstand life's storms.

The foolish man, however, takes no time to count the cost and builds anywhere he wants. His foundation is unstable—a mixture of airy philosophies and sand. In the middle of a storm, his house collapses with a crash and disappears beneath the deluge. Without a solid foundation, standing strong is impossible.

We won't know what is crooked unless we know what is straight.

If we are going to stand strong against authority abuse—if we plan to prevent it in our own lives—we must build our actions upon a solid, foundational understanding of godly authority. We won't know what is crooked unless we first know what is straight. We find our straight path, our solid foundation, when we answer this: "Where does godly authority come from?"

Do you remember why Jesus so amazed the Jews? *"The crowds were amazed at his teaching, because he taught as one who had authority, and not as their teachers of the law"* (Matthew 7:28–29 NIV). The Jews were amazed because they did not know where Jesus got His authority. He spoke and acted with such obvious power—but how? What was the source of His certainty, His sureness, His assertion that He had the say-so? It puzzled them so much that even the Jewish religious leaders admitted they did not understand.

> *Jesus entered the temple courts, and, while he was teaching, the chief priests and the elders of the people came to him. "By what authority are you doing these things?" they asked. "And who gave you this authority?"*
>
> (Matthew 21:23 NIV)

As I once heard Pastor Ray McCollum explain, we can find the answer to that question in a conversation between Jesus and a Roman centurion who, though a Gentile, was a devout and God-fearing man.

> *When Jesus had entered Capernaum, a centurion came to him, asking for help. "Lord," he said, "my servant lies at home paralyzed and in terrible suffering." Jesus said to him, "I will go and heal him." The centurion replied, "Lord, I do not deserve to have you come under my roof. But just say the word, and my servant will be healed. For I myself am a man under authority, with soldiers under me. I tell this one, 'Go,' and he goes; and that one, 'Come,' and he comes. I say to my servant, 'Do this,' and he does it."*
>
> (Matthew 8:5–9 NIV)

Notice that the centurion didn't say, "I, too, am a man who has authority." He told Jesus, *"I myself am a man* ***under*** *authority, with soldiers under me"* (v. 9, emphasis added).

He recognized that Jesus' power and authority was from the Father. Jesus had been sent by the Father and was in this sense a *delegate* for the Father.

As Romans 13:1 explains, true authority is given only by God:

> *Everyone must submit himself to the governing authorities, for there is no authority except that which God has established. The authorities that exist have been established by God.* (NIV)

The book of Genesis tells us that, from the start, God set some parts of His creation over others:

> *Then God said, "Let us make man in our image, in our likeness, and let them rule over the fish of the sea and the birds of the air, over the livestock, over all the earth, and over all the creatures that move along the ground."*
>
> (Genesis 1:26 NIV)

As Scripture records, God continued this precedent of putting some in authority over others. Man, for instance, was given authority over woman (Ephesians 5:22–23); kings and presidents authority over countrymen (2 Chronicles 9:8); and pastors authority over congregations (2 Corinthians 13:10).

Because God has established these authority relationships, they ought to reflect His character. That's why, after telling women to submit to their husbands, Paul exhorted husbands to imitate Christ: *"Husbands, love your wives, just as Christ loved the church and gave himself up for her"* (Ephesians 5:25 NIV). All authority must mirror the character of its Creator.

What's It For?

Genesis 2:15 says, *"The LORD God took the man and put him in the Garden of Eden to work it and take care of it"* (NIV).

This is the first time God put man in authority over anything. Notice that it is one of the very first things He did with His universe; while a "new creation" smell still lingered in the air, God posted a "Man at Work" sign and stepped back.

In that perfect, flawless time and place, the institution of godly authority followed God's design. It demonstrated this unshakable truth: Godly authority, without exception, nurtures and cultivates whatever is placed under it.

Godly authority always nurtures.

This truth applies to all kinds of authority in all kinds of relationships: in marriages, in churches, in the home, and in the workplace.

As my wife and I wrote in *Crazy House, Sane House*, for instance, a husband is responsible not only for caring for his wife, but also for encouraging her to grow in her strengths and gifts.

Why? Because a husband has authority over his wife. And just as God intended Adam to nurture and cultivate the garden placed in his care, God expects man to encourage his wife as well.

A woman should thus submit to her husband; God intends for her life to be led, fed, and nurtured by her husband so that it bears beautiful fruit.

This principle of encouragement extends to the church and to business contexts, as well. If the person in authority over you has an open hand, there's nothing you won't be able to do. Like a loving father, he should be happy—even excited—to support you in whatever God calls you to do.

Why? Because godly authority is selfless, desiring those under it to blossom and grow. Thus, those who exercise godly authority never feel threatened by their "children" but rather rejoice in their accomplishments.

We teach our children that police officers are their friends—(even though the sight of police cruisers parked along the highway makes us uncomfortable)—and that if they are ever lost, they should ask a police officer for help.

Godly authority looks out for the good of the governed.

Why? Because that police officer, that person of authority, that person who's "in charge," is a guarantee to every law-abiding citizen that when you need help, you have on your side the best your government has to offer.

Godly authority is always looking out for the good of those it governs and protects.

When authority looks out for those under it, the "ruled" have a greater incentive to respond with obedience to the guidelines intended for their good.

When driving, I try to keep my highway speed within the posted speed limit. This way, I don't feel a guilty jolt of adrenaline whenever I round a corner and see a police car. Instead of stomping on the brake pedal, hoping I can slow down before the officer scans me, I simply motor on my way.

In fact, seeing a police car makes me more confident because I know I don't have to worry about a crazy driver barreling down behind me at 90 miles per hour. He would have to get past the police officer there, who would exercise his authority to keep me safe. That's godly authority with a gun! (See Romans 13:3–4.)

As a pastor, I understand firsthand that I have similar responsibilities. As a husband is responsible for nurturing and encouraging his wife, a pastor is responsible for leading and encouraging his congregation. As a policeman cares for the well-being of citizens, a pastor must care for the spiritual well-being of his congregation.

There are many responsibilities that accompany my office. Like all pastors, I sometimes miss the mark; I have come to realize that some of our greatest successes come out of our worst failures.

When we fail, though, we must be willing to admit our mistakes, learn from them, and strive for greater God-centered maturity. It's when we make excuses for ourselves that our Christian life starts to stagnate—and we start abusing our authority.

In Ephesians 4, Paul outlined the various ministries in a church:

> *And He Himself gave some to be apostles, some prophets, some evangelists, and some pastors and teachers, for the equipping of the saints for the work of ministry, for the edifying of the body of Christ, till we all come to the unity of the faith and of the knowledge of the Son of God, to a perfect man, to the measure of the stature of the fullness of Christ.* (vv. 11–13)

We've heard these Scriptures so many times that we almost don't hear them at all any more; they just patter away in the background like the music played in department stores.

But what do they mean? God's Word deserves more than a passing glance. Let's take a deeper look at these verses by focusing on the office of pastor.

As the job of a shepherd is to tend his sheep, the job of a pastor (which literally means "shepherd") is to tend his flock—a flock given to him by the Lord. Remember, when Peter said he loved the Lord, Jesus replied, "Feed my sheep." As a spiritual overseer, the pastor is to look after, teach, and empower the people in his church. According to Ephesians 4, the office of pastor was given for three specific reasons:

1. The Perfecting of the Saints

I believe the word *"perfecting"* here refers to sanctification. Sanctification is the work of the Holy Spirit by which our human nature is transformed, through a lifelong process encompassing the whole of man's being, into greater Christlikeness.

As a pastor, I have both the authority and the responsibility to present my people with God's Word, an essential element in the sanctification process.

I should give them a balanced understanding of what Scripture teaches—mercy and judgment, grace and conviction—and if I do my job correctly, they will be armed with scriptural truth for every situation.

And if they don't know what God's Word says about a particular issue, they will know how to find out.

The Holy Spirit is responsible for sanctification but occasionally chooses to accomplish it through human tools. I must let the Holy Spirit do His work and I will do mine; God will not do my job, and I cannot do His.

2. The Work of the Ministry

In spite of their shortcomings, good pastors lead by example to bring laborers into effective ministry work—meeting people's needs, correcting congregants when necessary, and leading others to Christ. I cannot expect my congregation to understand Christian service unless I model it for them.

That is why, no matter the kind of outreach or function we do, chances are good that Bishop Bloomer will be there at some point, dressed up or with sleeves rolled up, depending on the occasion.

3. The Edifying of the Body of Christ

To edify someone is to build him up; this requires reliable, godly, and positive input.

A pastor can't build up his congregation unless he's *involved.* Part of being in authority is being in contact with the people God has placed under your care. This takes time, energy, patience, and sacrifice.

Years ago, a minister shared this story:

> A few months ago, I called an elders' meeting. We had a radio program, and it always concluded by giving people a phone number they could call if they wanted prayer. We had recently made the decision

to conserve the resources of our staff by putting a dedicated answering machine on that line. So when I called this meeting and told the elders that I was going to play a recording from our prayer line, they were excited. But instead of hearing the good report they expected, they sat in stunned silence as we listened to the monotone voice of a young woman.

"I'm committing suicide. I've been looking for a reason not to, but I decided I was going to do it tonight. I called, 'cause I thought maybe you could give me a reason not to. But now I know there's no God, so I'm going to do it. Goodbye."

Not every ministry can operate a prayer line or supply someone full time to answer it; and not every pastor can minister full time, either—some work to support families, as I did starting out.

> Being under authority means giving up some of your rights.

As the title to the book by Mac Anderson and Lance Wubbels wisely says, *To a Child Love Is Spelled T-I-M-E.* At the very least, a godly authority always has time for the people it guides and leads.

I do everything possible to make my office and staff members completely approachable for my congregation. I feel that anyone who has a problem, who has been hurt, or who feels the need to confront me about something should have the opportunity to be heard.

I cannot overstate the importance of honest communication between spiritual authorities and the people over whom they wield authority. I not only tell the people in my congregation to talk to me whenever they needed to, but I also tell them, "If you're so mad that you're on the brink of shouting, do it! I need to hear it; I need to know that you are that upset."

How will I help them, how can I love them, if they are afraid to be themselves in front of me?

But Why?

We've basically come back to where we started: godly authority will nurture and cultivate whatever is placed under it.

But there's more to authority than that—isn't there? If authority was nothing more than taking care of people, we could have an *absence* of authority but no real *abuse* of authority.

Our problems come, however, from the fact that at the core of authority, one person is required to submit his or her decision-making ability to another.

In a sense, being under authority means giving up some of your rights. Why would God ask us to do that?

Well, imagine for a moment a world in which there was no authority, where no one was required to follow rules set by anyone else. Would you feel safe driving down the road with no speed limit to keep fellow drivers in check? What if you couldn't count on anyone else to stop at red lights or stop signs?

Would you be worried if your local gun store sold automatic firearms to known murderers? (And the murderers wouldn't even be felons because nobody would have the authority to say they were doing wrong!)

Eventually we would be living under rules made by other people, but not because anyone was rightfully in charge; the strong would simply force the weak into submission.

As the strong fought among themselves for more control and power, anarchy would ensue. This is why civilized people have established systems of authority (government) to which they have voluntarily submitted for centuries.

On a smaller scale, think about how a warehouse for a large business works. Imagine that no one was in charge of the warehouse. Some of the less motivated workers would perhaps spend the bulk of their day by the coffee maker and would happily collect their paycheck for drinking coffee.

In the garden of Eden, God and man both had authority.

Problems would arise among the more motivated workers, too. What if one guy thought the product should be organized alphabetically while someone else thought it should be organized by color?

There would be no rules to follow and no one to make the rules; most of their time would be spent arguing about how things should be sorted or working to take each other's systems apart.

It wasn't always this way. In the garden of Eden both God and man had authority that was used entirely for nurturing the things under them. In God's perfect plan, mankind did what was best because he was motivated by love for God and His creation, not because he was restrained by rules.

In fact, there was only one rule in the entire universe for man to follow at that time, a rule God laid down to protect us: do not partake of fruit from the Tree of the Knowledge of Good and Evil. (See Genesis 2:16–17.)

God-given authority exists to protect us from ourselves.

Knowing good from evil (in other words, knowing that evil even *exists*) makes us responsible for choosing between good and evil, and this choice is a burden God did not want us to have to carry. God loved us so much, though, that He wanted pure, voluntary love in return.

This forced God to face a dilemma: to let us choose Him, He had to offer us a choice between Him and something else. The problem was that everything good was already contained in Him! The only choice He could offer us was between Himself and death. In foolish arrogance, the race of man decided it should choose "independence" from God even though this choice meant death and destruction.

The moment that man chose to break the *one rule* God had established, human nature became twisted for all time.

God-given authority exists now for one simple reason: to protect us from ourselves. That's why a man has a pastor over him—to help him keep his life in line with God's Word. That's why a woman has her husband over her—to serve as the executive member in their partnership. That's why children have parents over them—to raise them in fear and admonition of the Lord.

Remember what the centurion said about authority in Matthew 5? Authority is a thing delegated from above, God's protective direction that filters down a chain of people who are ultimately all accountable to Him.

Good Leadership Maintains Godly Authority

Good leadership is invaluable. Not only does it help promote success in the everyday lives of others, but it also helps to birth other good leaders.

Good leaders know how to develop the potential of others, not suppress it.

In fact, the best path to follow in your pursuit of success is that of a good leader. When you are attempting to reach a goal, it is always wise to seek out individuals who have already succeeded in that particular area.

Qualities of Good Leaders

1. They know how to bring out the best in those around them.
2. They are good teachers.
3. They do not mind divulging some of the secrets to their success.
4. They deserve and receive the respect of their peers.
5. They practice what they preach, following the advice they give to others in their own lives.

6. They are able to admit when they are wrong and are willing to take the necessary steps to correct their mistakes.

7. They are disciplined and committed to completing whatever tasks they are assigned to undertake.

Under the tutelage of a good, strong leader, the sky is the limit.

With weak leadership, however, you continually find yourself constrained from realizing and reaching your full potential.

The success I enjoy today is largely attributable to the fact that I surrounded myself with good leaders who were willing to teach me without limiting my strengths. I feel that I have always been a leader, though I did not always use my leadership skills to promote positive achievements in my life.

Early on, I lacked many of the qualities and disciplines required for honing one's latent leadership abilities.

When I began to educate myself, however, I learned to emulate the positive attributes of powerful men who were good leaders. I then began learning how to excel in my strengths and correct my weaknesses in order to seize my destiny.

If you think that you have to be a natural-born leader in order to lead properly, think again. Many of the greatest leaders in our society started off as scrawny, timid kids who lingered constantly in the background in order to hide their insecurities.

At one time or another, however, we all receive an epiphany that gives a glimpse of our innate abilities. Though the image lasts only for a moment, it lasts a lifetime within our minds. It is this image that leaders grasp as their inspiration while reaching toward their goals.

The Making of a Great Leader

Leaders don't make excuses; they make decisions. When things are not going as planned, leaders decide to make some much-needed changes. When things are going well, leaders use that time to continue improving themselves instead of sitting back with lackadaisical complacency.

So, how do you become a great leader? Here are a few pointers to get you on the right path:

1. Have a vision. Be clear and concise concerning what you want so that when you discuss it with others, your passion pulls them into it instead of turning them off. Also, be sure to make room in your vision for future growth. Don't ever become so complacent that you fail to consider the changing of the times. Pay attention to what is going on around you.

2. Be honest concerning your weaknesses and be prepared to make sacrifices in order to overcome them.

3. Listen to others who have made great accomplishments and study their techniques. Become a careful listener. Learn from their mistakes as well as their achievements.

4. Stay focused. Welcome constructive criticism, but shy away from critical people who point out weak points without offering advice or support.

5. If something intimidates you, don't run from it. Instead, conquer it with study and preparation.

6. Learn how to prioritize and arrange your life accordingly. If you find yourself continually starting new projects without finishing old ones, this is an indicator that you need to reorganize and prioritize your goals. All too often, people waste time thinking about a vision instead taking the necessary steps to bring it to pass.

7. As you are rising to the top, maintain your integrity. Many people make the mistake of using ungodly methods while climbing the ladder to success; by the time they reach the top, no one is there to say, "Congratulations." Other people are even going so far as to compromise their godly beliefs in exchange for wealth. Matthew 16:26 warns, *"For what profit is it to a man if he gains the whole world, and loses his own soul? Or what will a man give in exchange for his soul?"* In all that you do, keep God first.

8. Build credibility. "Mean what you say, and say what you mean." If you develop a reputation of being unreliable and untrustworthy, it becomes increasingly difficult for you to expand beyond the "glass ceiling" that you are unknowingly creating for yourself.

9. Get to know the people around you. I have found that some of the greatest leaders are not

the "untouchables" but are rather those who take the time to get to know the people around them. In spite of their fortune or fame, they do not forget to consider the needs of those whom they have employed, the customers they service, the parishioners who come to hear them weekly, and so on.

10. Pay attention to detail. Always strive to do more than what is expected and you will receive above and beyond what you were trying to achieve.

3

THE MAKING OF AN AUTHORITY ABUSER

Pride goes before destruction, and a haughty spirit before a fall.
Proverbs 16:18

He was called the Morning Star, the most beautiful creature ever created. His very movements were music, and he led one-third of the heavenly host in a symphony of worship to the Almighty. He had been delegated authority second only to God's, and he shone with the very glory that radiated from the Father's throne.

His name was Lucifer. You know his story: Lucifer looked at the power and brilliance that were his, and his heart lifted up with pride. He decided he would make himself equal with God—and for his rebellion, God threw him out of heaven.

I know what you're thinking: *How could Lucifer have been so crazy?* He had the universe by the tail and then ruined it all! How did he ever end up envying God? Was Lucifer *drunk,* for goodness' sake?

Actually, that's not a bad analogy. You see, the way I understand it, authority is like liquor—and Lucifer had more to "drink" than was good for him.

Lucifer had rightful, God-given authority, but he made one critical mistake: he forgot he hadn't earned the authority and splendor he was holding.

> Authority can be as intoxicating as liquor.

When he forgot this, he began to resent the fact that he didn't command the same kind of respect as God. *After all,* he must have thought, *my glory is nearly as brilliant as His.*

The intoxicating liquor of authority went to his head, and he began thinking and acting in ways he would not have done had he been sober and in his right mind.

Now, don't misunderstand: rebellion against God is always wrong, always sinful, and never justifiable.

Had Lucifer known what to guard himself against, though, and had he realized the intoxicating effects of authority ahead of time, perhaps he would not have fallen into the sin that will ultimately destroy him and the spirits under him.

Lucifer established a pattern followed by every abuser of authority from that time until today. For one thing, authority abuse only springs up where there is a middleman—someone between God and the person being ruled over.

That doesn't narrow things down much; as we discussed in the previous chapter, all parents, pastors, and employers occupy a position of authority because God delegated it to them.

I think it's worth mentioning, though, that abuse shows up frequently in *human* chains of command—say, an associate pastor who comes between the senior pastor and the church members.

There are many reasons for this, the biggest reason being that people in these middleman positions have been "drinking" authority for a much shorter period of time than people in senior leadership positions. Many times, they just can't quite hold their "liquor" yet.

As they start growing tipsy with their newfound authority, these abusers succumb to the most natural inclination in the world—the desire for another "drink"! Pretty soon, priorities get misplaced, and these leaders start focusing on what will advance them in the eyes of those in authority over them.

This self-centered focus—pride—is precisely what led Lucifer to rebel against God. By the time a person is this "drunk" on authority, he no longer cares about the purpose for which he received authority in the first place.

A prideful spirit can provoke rebellion.

As Lucifer forgot all about leading others in the worship of Jehovah, an associate pastor may stop truly caring about the ministries he oversees. Whether he admits it (even to himself), he will start serving himself at the expense of those under him. Let me tell you a story as an example:

> One weekend, most of our leadership team (myself included) left town to attend an out-of-state retreat. We left the care of the church and planning for the

Sunday service in the very capable hands of a young man raised up under our ministry. On Sunday, one of our young women led the worship, and this young man presented the sermon followed by a time of ministry at the altar.

Everything went smoothly until he began to take a special offering at the service's end. (We were in the middle of a building project at the time and would collect a special offering for the construction project every Sunday.) This week, as the time of offering began, a number of people got up and walked out.

Now, our congregation has never walked out on me while I was taking an offering, and I imagine that is what stung this young man's pride. The authority he had been drinking all morning went to his head, and he no longer acted the way the young man I know and love would have acted if he were sober.

"Shut the doors," he told the ushers. "Everyone can stay until we've finished taking this offering."

The ushers moved to comply, but they had half a family inside the church, half already out, and a handful of people were returning from the rest-room as well, so the ushers waited several minutes in an effort to sort out the flow of people before shutting the doors.

My young friend started yelling from the pulpit, scolding the ushers for not shutting the doors when he told them to. "Wasn't I speaking English?" he demanded.

> When I returned from my trip, a friend from a partner church called to tell me about the incident. The people who had tried to leave were visitors from his church, and they had stood to leave during the offering because they had to pack for an early afternoon flight. Since they weren't members of this particular congregation, they hadn't thought anything of slipping out during the closing offering for the building fund.

Obviously, the way my associate minister conducted himself constituted an abuse of the authority I delegated to him. He did and said things I would never have done, and he was motivated by self-interest.

At the time, though, he had no idea he was being abusive. It sneaked up on him like one drink too many—the one that pushed him over the edge from a warm "drinking glow" to intoxication.

In this situation, he was no better—and certainly no worse—than any other authority abuser. The road from stewardship to abuse is always the same, marked with snares and deceptions along the way.

When challenged about their dogmatic style, abusive leaders often dismiss the serious nature of their actions and give a list of reasons to justify them.

Usually they describe their dictatorship as "caring so much for the people," and often they are as deceived as the people who follow them, sincerely believing they are responsible for holiness in the lives of their parishioners.

Normal people are stubborn and weak, the pastor concludes; in order for them to live a life of godliness and holiness, he figures he must rule his congregation with an iron fist of authority.

This doesn't always happen all at once. Often, a pastor starts his ministry full of fire and enthusiasm, hoping to encourage his people to become the most dynamic Christians since the day of Pentecost.

> Pastors should not try to do God's job for Him.

All too often, though, he becomes discouraged when people fail to become transformed as quickly as he would prefer. His sermons become more and more overburdened with instruction as he aims to make his people see the high calling of God.

The more time passes, the less content the pastor is to wait for God to change the people. In his self-imposed frustration, the pastor eventually forgets all about pointing people toward God and begins feeling personally responsible for the way they live their lives.

He starts holding several church services a week just to keep people in church and "out of trouble" and holds his congregation to a standard so strict that he doesn't even make his own family comply with it. In short, he becomes a tyrant.

When a man does this—when he tries to do God's job for Him—it's no surprise that he soon feels overburdened. After trying every tactic he can think of, he grows bitter when things don't change. *Not only do these people refuse to change their lives,* he thinks, *but they don't even appreciate how hard I work to keep them right with God.* And the truth is, he's right! Nobody appreciates the way he abuses his authority;

everyone resents him, even as they follow him away from God's will.

This pattern holds true no matter where you find an authority abuser. The person in authority starts out wanting the best for those under him but ends up resenting those same people.

Even in the case of the most malicious authority abuse ever, I believe that the abuser, in his heart of hearts, doesn't really like being abusive; this is not who God created him to be. The abuser is trapped in the lie just as surely as a drunken man gets trapped in his confused state.

The tragic and ironic part of the whole thing is that, with his controlling grasp, the abuser sacrifices the one thing that could really help him be a catalyst for change in his followers' lives.

Look at these Scriptures:

> *Then He called his twelve disciples together and gave them power and authority over all demons, and to cure diseases.* (Luke 9:1)

> *Behold, I give you the authority to trample on serpents and scorpions, and over all the power of the enemy, and nothing shall by any means hurt you.* (Luke 10:19)

As these verses show, every believer has been given spiritual authority over the rulers of darkness and the ability to change history's course. This is why it is so sad when someone trades that God-granted power for ungodly possessiveness. It is because we don't realize our power that our lives plateau into a state of stagnation.

The result? People go about weekly religious rituals with no anointing, naming and claiming things that God never intended them to have in the first place, misplacing priorities, and missing their God-given destiny.

What (Not) to Do

Paul wrote this to the Philippians while he was being held in a dungeon in Rome:

> *Therefore, my beloved, as you have always obeyed, not as in my presence only, but now much more in my absence, work out your own salvation with fear and trembling; for it is God who works in you both to will and to do for His good pleasure.* (Philippians 2:12–13)

Paul knew it was not his *presence* that would keep the Philippians walking after God but rather his *absence,* along with their ability to develop true relationships with the Father. It would be *those* relationships—the ones between God and each Philippian believer—that would provoke their wills to do God's *"good pleasure."*

If it is not in a person to do the will of God, obey His voice, and operate under His command, no amount of browbeating will save him. The only change he might make is hiding his undisciplined behavior from the person trying to control him. That's how a person learns to fear earthly authority more than he or she fears God.

Any time a man is feared more than God, idolatry is present—and God has said, *"I, the Lord your God, am a jealous God"* (Exodus 20:5). He will not share His glory, for He alone is supreme; none is to be feared except Him.

Every pastor should have this truth branded on his heart: "There is nothing I can do to whip a person into shape if he is determined to walk after the flesh."

Individuals must go through their own experiences in life that will ultimately draw the defining line of who they are and which paths they will take. Those who walk after the Spirit are convicted when they are in error and seek to right the things that have gone wrong; it is the Spirit who convicts, though—not the pastor.

When a person has an intimate relationship with God, his spirit becomes less accessible to outside voices that seek to steer him in the opposite direction of God's designs.

> Fearing men more than God constitutes idolatry.

In contrast, beating on people with condemnation is a human tactic of control. It is not biblical, and even Jesus' ministry did not operate out of condemnation. *"For God sent not his Son into the world to condemn the world; but that the world through him might be saved"* (John 3:17 KJV).

Imagine you are driving along peaceably in your car and you see a police officer with a car pulled over. The driver, still inside the car, has license and registration in hand.

The police officer is throwing a fit, stomping back and forth alongside the car, banging on the car roof. He's red in the face, and he's screaming at the top of his lungs:

"You were going fifteen miles an hour over the speed limit! FIFTEEN! Do you know how fast that is? You should be ashamed of yourself! How many times do I have to tell you to drive slower than the posted speed limit?! But, noooooo, you have to drive FIFTEEN MILES AN HOUR OVER! I work so hard, trying to keep these streets safe; I talk to you, I give you tickets, and I keep telling you you're going to jail if you don't change your ways! Why? Why do I have to tell you over and over...?"

Jesus' ministry did not condemn.

Now, that little scene is a tad scary because it's definitely authority abuse. But I bet that you think it's more funny than scary. Why?

It's probably because all that screaming is a sure sign that the police officer feels helpless and out of control.

Think about it: when most police officers approach a lawbreaker, their voices are calm and their motions unhurried. They have the power of the entire government behind them and they know it.

It would be completely ridiculous for a police officer to feel personally slighted when someone breaks the speed limit because the law is much bigger than any one man. In fact, it is when police officers begin taking the actions of lawbreakers as personal offenses that we see instances of police brutality and other abuses of the legal system.

Now, apply this lesson to the big picture of life. What are we forced to conclude when we find a parent screaming at her children, nagging and belittling them, or a husband criticizing his wife, finding fault with all she does?

What about a pastor who paces his platform like a wild animal, practically foaming at the mouth as he rails against his congregation's "sinfulness"?

That's right. One of the biggest reasons leaders abuse their authority is that they feel out of control—like they can't do their jobs right. And, as I said before, this feeling of impotence often arises when leaders try to do God's job.

Of course, they can't do His job because He doesn't *want* them to have that much control.

Still, they neglect their true spiritual responsibilities in the effort to succeed. Nobody's work gets done, and things ultimately collapse into a horrid jumble.

I honestly believe that if potential authority abusers would free themselves from the perceived responsibility that *they* must change people's lives, they would never become abusive. They would have the liberty to love people—even sinners—just the way they are, and they would help people take the "small steps," like understanding God's principles for finances.

A leader like that would soon begin seeing the cumulative effect of gradual, healthy growth in some of his people. The people who refuse to grow, then, would not seem like such a terrible blot on the record. The pastor would begin seeing how these things depend entirely on God.

The Even Darker Side

There is another cause of authority abuse, and it amounts to an unhealthy desire for power or influence. Often, abusers of this kind have been abused themselves or come from a background in which they were not valued as people.

You see, abuse breeds abuse. People who have been abused set out to "fix" themselves while unknowingly slipping into the habits and philosophies of the people who abused them. They approach life with fierce determination to be *somebody*, even though they never truly believe they are valuable.

Often, an abusive ministry is one that has either broken away from or been kicked out of an established church because the person who practices this type of abuse cannot tolerate being under authority; he must wield it. The abuser's hunger to be influential demands that he occupy a leadership position.

Sometimes he believes his humble background gives him a special perspective, as though he's "paid his dues"; sometimes he just needs to prove his importance.

Regardless of the reasons, though, he feels he needs a position of authority to attract and control people who have strong talents. He then uses these people as facilitators to sustain and advance his position of authority because he doesn't trust any of his own gifts or abilities. These facilitators help the authority abuser create an atmosphere of control.

Abuse breeds abuse.

Because he needs the gifts of other people, the abuser is normally terrified of losing control over others. He seeks ever-increasing authority in an awful, vicious cycle.

All people, even the wounded and hurting, have God-given gifts or talents. It takes little time for an authority abuser to learn that hurting people are almost pathetically eager to contribute their gifts in order to receive affirmation.

Thus, abusive ministries are often more sensitive than others to the needs and hurts of people at their services and better than many others at getting people involved in the church—not because they genuinely care but because they *need* the gifts these hurting people bring.

Abusers are afraid of losing control.

Authority abusers don't have the ability to nurture and refresh the people under them the way a leader should, and, eventually, their people grow tired and get used up.

When a person who is under authority abuse no longer has the emotional or spiritual energy to pour into the abuser's work, the abuser lets him fade into the background as fresh, newly grateful faces pick up the task of propping up the authority figure.

Alternatively, the "used-up" individual may be given a chance to commit himself completely and irrevocably to the abuser's ministry. If the individual is willing to totally forfeit producing anything on his own (by pouring everything into the abusive ministry), the abuser begins pouring back into him, grooming him for service.

Sometimes an abuser claims he is preparing this person to be sent out; in many cases, though, the truth is that nobody leaves.

Often, an authority abuser is surrounded by a small circle of codependent followers who live and die by his words. These facilitators are like the eunuchs with whom Queen Jezebel surrounded herself (see 2 Kings 9:32). Much more spiritual-looking than the rest of the congregation and more fervently defensive of the ministry, they have been spiritually "castrated" and can reproduce only vicariously through the ministry of the abuser.

The worst of it is that abuse almost always propagates itself.

I once knew a boy whose parents both worked all day long. His father was an abusive alcoholic. Every morning after his parents left for work, this boy was responsible for waking his siblings, packing their lunches, feeding them breakfast, and sending them to school.

Then he had to pack his own lunch and go to school. After school he was required to clean the house and prepare dinner so it was mostly ready and waiting when his parents came home late in the evening. If he failed to have things just right, he could count on being beaten by his father.

Abuse usually propagates itself.

Now, how do you suppose this boy treated his siblings? The fact is, he was abusive. He wasn't as abusive as his father, but he used his authority to save his skin, to make his siblings his helpers, and, occasionally, to turn his siblings into targets for the pain and anger he couldn't vent elsewhere. The simple truth: abuse breeds abuse.

Imagine a situation in which a church leader was found to be guilty of adultery. There is no doubt that he would be wrong and in sin, and scriptural discipline would be administered.

Suppose, though, that the discipline brought him to a place of real repentance, but that the authority over him refused to restore him to Christian fellowship as the apostle Paul instructed. (See 1 Corinthians 5:1–3; 2 Corinthians 2:5–8.)

That would constitute an abuse of authority, and Paul said it could cause the repentant man to *"be swallowed up with overmuch sorrow"* (2 Corinthians 2:7 KJV).

> Pride is the root of most authority abuse.

I have seen this happen and I know what results from it. I have seen men leave the churches that would not restore them to start their own ministries elsewhere.

They become the kind of people we talked about at the beginning of this section: distrustful of all authority but their own, surrounding themselves only with people who will help boost them toward their desires, abusing others in an effort to feel valuable.

In Sum

If you could distill the causes of authority abuse down to their most elemental level, you would find at the bottom of your beaker an old and familiar enemy: the sin of pride.

Don't think I am talking about arrogance; for most authority abusers, arrogance comes much, much later in the game.

When I speak of pride, I am speaking of the simple (and, in our fallen state, very natural) inclination to think of ourselves before thinking of others. Or, if you'd rather, it's our inclination to *prefer* our own interests over the interests of those around us.

AUTHORITY *Abusers*

There is hardly a soul that hasn't wished at one time that he could hold in his hands real power, if only for a moment, to set the world the way he thinks it should be.

Authority abuse is what happens when someone acquires this power and uses it without prudent reverence. It is, in fact, the worst kind of irreverence—a disregard for the Creator's right to have His handiwork, or people, treated with honor.

Abusers always have a need to exalt themselves—they'll even attempt to steal the glory of God in the process. They have an all-about-me mentality that allows no one within the confines of their space to detract from their presence.

The behavior of abusers is a form of insecurity disguised as confidence. Abusers must maintain a façade of friendliness in order to keep from being exposed as oppressors. The question is, how are so many caught in the snares of the abuser?

Those people who are most prone to becoming authority abusers tend to have a number of things in common: (1) they may suffer from low self-esteem, (2) they may have witnessed or experienced abuse at a young age, and (3) they are unable to resist authority figures.

4

The Making of a Victim of Authority Abuse

It is better to trust in the Lord *than to put confidence in man.*
Psalm 118:8

Here is a true story that will give you a better understanding of what makes someone vulnerable to authority abuse:

After being offered a promising career in public relations, Julianne moved from her small hometown in North Carolina to the Big Apple—New York City—to complete her studies and advance her career.

It wasn't long before Julianne would meet Patrick, who became a close confidant. He was also able to shed some light on many of the questions concerning God and spiritual matters that had plagued Julianne for some time.

Patrick soon suggested that she accompany him to church, and she graciously complied. As their relationship flourished and they became "more than just friends," Julianne began to notice subtle changes in Patrick's character. He raised objections to her wardrobe, her makeup, and her spending habits; he inquired about her new friends and acquaintances, and so forth.

At first, Julianne was smitten with Patrick's concerned and protective nature, and she simply assured him that their relationship was secure. As time went on, the two of them began studying the pastor's sermons each week after visiting Patrick's church. After hearing a message on the topic of submission, Julianne's world became utterly consumed with submitting to and pleasing Patrick.

She clung to every word that came across the pulpit regarding relationships, and when the pastor preached a message to singles based on 1 Corinthians 7:9—*"...if they cannot exercise self-control, let them marry. For it is better to marry than to burn with passion"*—Julianne finally decided to accept Patrick's marriage proposal.

Although she had her reservations, the couple was advised by the pastor that they needed to either hurry up and get married or end the relationship, and Julianne decided that she did not want to continue doing anything that displeased God.

She and Patrick set a date; days later, they were married in the pastor's study.

Only a few weeks into the marriage, Julianne received a shocking phone call that wakened her to the reality of her situation.

"Hello?" she answered the phone hesitantly, not recognizing the number displayed on the caller ID.

"Hi, is this the new wife of Patrick?"

"Who's asking?"

"This is Marcia."

"Marcia. Who?"

"Patrick's current wife," the voice on the other end responded.

"Oh, I'm sorry, you must have the wrong number."

"No. I'm sure I do not."

Sure enough, Patrick was indeed still married to Marcia, his first wife. Though the two of them had been separated for two years, they still kept in close contact with one another, and Marcia was furious that Patrick would marry another woman while he was still married to her.

In her anger, Marcia picked up the phone and called Patrick's house to enlighten his new wife with this invaluable information.

Julianne replayed the picture again and again in her mind, saying to herself, *I thought I'd done everything right. I even consulted the pastor before getting married.*

> Then it hit her. All of the warning signs had been present, but Julianne realized that she had become a victim of scriptural manipulation.
>
> Not wanting to displease God, she married a man who displeased her instead. *Hurry up and get married or end the relationship* were the last words she remembered before committing to ruin her life.

I remember the first time Julianne visited my office for a counseling session after she had ended her relationship with Patrick and returned to North Carolina.

Not only was she distraught because of the deception in the relationship, but she also had a question that she wanted me to clarify. Weeping and broken, she said, "I trusted this pastor with my spiritual life and my husband with my soul. How could two people at once betray that trust with such little sorrow?"

I responded that the only person to whom you should entrust your spirit is God, and He is also the only One to whom you should give away your soul.

> God is the only One to whom you should give away your soul.

So troubled was Julianne with the rude awakening of her situation that by the time she'd gotten to our church, she'd had several nervous breakdowns and was on the verge of giving up entirely.

Because her deception occurred during a time when Julianne was searching for God, she was even more susceptible to scripturally weak teachings and tactics of manipulation.

And although her story does have a pleasant ending—she was able to bounce back and enjoy a nice life—not everyone is as fortunate after being the victim of religious deception.

People have been known to blame God and embrace the demonic as a means of releasing their anger about bad advice or corrupt counsel that they received from the church.

When individuals relinquish their *entire* life into the hands of human frailty, they are destined to experience disappointment and failure. Wherever deception is involved, it is driven by the spirit of iniquity and deceit.

Do Not Make the Same Mistakes

Any time you are being guided to engage in an activity that conflicts with (1) the truth of God's Word, (2) your conscience, or (3) your godly desires, always know that manipulation is at work.

Julianne overlooked major signs that should never be discounted when making a life-altering decision such as marriage.

1. Making Excuses for Warning Signs

Julianne made excuses for the warning signs. God always forewarns us.

Even when people say, "I had no idea," after a few minutes of interrogation, they come to realize, "Wow, I saw that, or I saw this, but I didn't think anything of it."

Never ignore the signs. They are all worth investigating when it comes to making a decision that's going to alter the rest of your life. For instance, if you are being coaxed into a marriage instead of entering into it willingly, you are destined to see the true nature of the relationship—but many times it is after the nuptial vows have been recited.

2. Losing Focus

Julianne lost her focus.

I often tell people not to make too many permanent decisions in temporary locations.

Julianne was sent to New York to advance her career.

By meeting up with the wrong individuals, however, she was forced to start over from scratch as her life took a dramatic U-turn.

3. Failing to Consider the Source

Julianne failed to consider the source. After knowing Patrick's pastor for only a few weeks, Julianne placed her entire spiritual well-being in his hands.

Leaders are meant to lead and guide us toward God's truth, not to become gods to us.

4. Placing Everyone Else's Needs First

Julianne placed everyone else's needs before her own.

There is something about authority abusers that allows them to notice gentle-hearted individuals a mile away.

They prey on these people in order to flaunt their haughtiness and hide their own insecurities.

Because Julianne was so willing to place the needs of everyone else before her own, she became the sacrificial lamb that was slain in the name of false teachings.

5

Recognizing Authority Abuse

He who says, "I know Him," and does not keep His commandments, is a liar, and the truth is not in him.
1 John 2:4

It can be difficult to identify abusive leaders, especially if you're involved in the situation. They resemble predators in many ways, and they remind me of spiders, in particular.

Having no teeth, spiders cannot break down food for themselves, so they spin beautiful webs to trap passing insects instead.

Once a spider has caught an insect, it sucks out the bug's protein- and nutrient-rich juices, draining it until it is dead and dry.

Now, insects are incredibly strong for their size; a spider couldn't simply begin bleeding one of them to death without getting mauled, especially since spiders often victimize insects that are actually stronger and more powerful than they are.

How do spiders do it? They are equipped with a kind of poison, a special nerve toxin that paralyzes the victim's ability to resist but leaves it alive so that its life juices can be extracted easily.

It is something similar to this paralyzing toxin that makes authority abusers so hard to recognize. They are always deceitful and manipulative; no one announces, "I am abusing you right now, but you have to obey me anyway."

Rather, they act concerned about the welfare of the people they are using and may even use that "worry" as a lever for emotional blackmail.

Their victims rarely have more than a vague sense that something is not exactly "right"—and the abusers always make sure the victims conclude it's their own fault.

Authority abuse stems from people of all ages, races, and ethnic backgrounds.

It crosses geographical locations, lacks favor, is void of conscience, and frees itself of regret for its actions.

Authority abusers can be hard to recognize.

It can be invoked mentally, physically, or emotionally, yet its motives remain the same: to subdue and control the object of its aggression for selfish gain.

Rarely do abusers identify themselves upon initial contact.

On the contrary, they often present themselves as very caring, sensitive, and benevolent individuals who are willing to lend a hand to those who are in need. This guise of goodwill is often what keeps victims from escaping the abuser's web of deceit—blinded by the abuser's apparent benevolence, they may remain in the abusive relationship long after the true nature of the abuser has been revealed.

These victims cannot see past the kindness that was once shown and accept the true character of the abuser.

Scripture is often used to keep victims bound.

There are usually subtle signs that we often overlook—especially in Christendom—that expose the true character of an authority abuser.

Abusers will use whatever weakness they can find to control their victims.

Unfortunately, it is Scripture that many abusers use to keep their victims bound.

The very thing that should bring believers joy is perverted and mishandled to invoke control and cause anguish.

Faced with questions about their tactics, abusers will react with responses such as, *"Touch not mine anointed, and do my prophets no harm"* (1 Chronicles 16:22 KJV).

They twist Scripture in order to continue the cycle of abuse, rejecting confrontation and rarely providing an answer of accountability for their actions.

Regardless of abusers' elusiveness, there are specific telltale signs that always expose the abusers for who they truly are.

Signs of an Abuser

1. He or she becomes overly intrusive in the personal lives of others.

2. He or she constantly points out or reinforces others' weaknesses, making them believe that they cannot live a healthy or prosperous life independent of the abuser.

3. He or she continually reminds the victim and others of all the "good" or benevolent acts that he or she has performed on the victim's behalf.

4. He or she makes excuses for improper words and actions instead of apologizing for them.

5. He or she blames others for personal flaws and imperfections.

6. He or she belittles others while constantly speaking well of himself or herself.

7. He or she is extremely territorial and envies the accomplishments of others.

8. He or she requires victims to consult him or her and obtain permission before they make a decision.

9. He or she puts personal wants and needs before everything—and everyone—else.

10. He or she uses manipulation and intimidation to control others.

Recalling the Past

I know of a young lady who grew up in an abusive household. She was very bright and an excellent student; after high school, she went on to a prestigious private college with a major in education.

It wasn't until her second year, while she was studying child development, that she realized she had been verbally and emotionally abused her entire life. She had always thought what went on in her household was normal, because her spirit was paralyzed by the abuser's toxin.

If you need to ask yourself and God, "Am I prey for a soul-sucking, spiritual spider?"

I have a very simple definition of authority abuse that can help you answer that question: *Authority abuse is any situation in which an authority figure's influence eclipses that of God's or disrupts God's divine order of authority.*

Of course, what is easy to say isn't always easy to see. I think it's time to talk about the demonic spirit behind most, if not all, instances of authority abuse.

In Revelation 2:18–29, Jesus addressed a church where this demonic spirit was at work among its people:

> *And to the angel of the church in Thyatira write, "These things says the Son of God, who has eyes like a flame of fire, and His feet like fine brass: 'I know your works, love, service, faith, and your patience; and as for your works, the last are more than the first. Nevertheless I have a few things against you, because you allow that woman Jezebel, who calls herself a prophetess, to teach and seduce My servants to commit sexual immorality and eat things sacrificed to idols. And I*

gave her time to repent of her sexual immorality, and she did not repent. Indeed I will cast her into a sickbed, and those who commit adultery with her into great tribulation, unless they repent of their deeds. I will kill her children with death, and all the churches shall know that I am He who searches the minds and hearts. And I will give to each one of you according to your works. Now to you I say, and to the rest in Thyatira, as many as do not have this doctrine, who have not known the depths of Satan, as they say, I will put on you no other burden. But hold fast what you have till I come. And he who overcomes, and keeps My works until the end, to him I will give power over the nations; he shall rule them with a rod of iron; they shall be dashed to pieces like the potter's vessels'; as I also have received from My Father; and I will give him the morning star. He who has an ear, let him hear what the Spirit says to the churches." (Revelation 2:18–29)

Jesus referred to a particular evil woman who was clearly in a place of influence as "Jezebel" because her behavior and the fruit that grew on the branches of her life was so much like the wickedness of the queen Jezebel we read about in the Old Testament. (See 1 Kings 16–21; 2 Kings 9.)

It appears this woman of Thyatira was acting under the influence of the same evil spirit, or the same kind of spirit, as Queen Jezebel of old—and with similar results.

To put it briefly, both "Jezebels" abused their authority with powerful use of deceit and manipulation.

In addition to teaching idolatry, the first Jezebel was also a candid murderer; and Jesus characterized the teaching of the second Jezebel as *"the depths of Satan."*

Who's Your Doorway to God?

Anyone who acts under the influence of the spirit that typified these two women invariably puts himself between God and the people under him.

I believe that any leader who stands between someone and God is vulnerable to the influence of the Jezebel spirit.

As I write this, the Roman Catholic Church is weathering yet another round of bad publicity because of a number of priests who have been found guilty of child molestation, a sin found in other churches as well. How were so many children manipulated and convinced to keep quiet about their horrible secrets?

Deceit obscures the real Authority.

The answer is this: To the children they abused, these priests represented God. In the nature of the Jezebel spirit, deceit and manipulation obscured the *real* Authority.

The most frightening thing about the abusive behavior engendered by the Jezebel spirit is that a person who dabbles in idolatry almost always ends up swallowed by it.

The commentators of the *NIV Study Bible* made this note about the Old Testament Jezebel and her husband, King Ahab: "The names of Ahab's sons (Ahazia, *'The LORD grasps;'* Joram, *'The LORD is exalted'*) suggest that Ahab did not intend to replace the worship of the Lord with the worship of Baal but to worship both deities in a syncretistic way."

In other words, when Ahab decided to make room for Jezebel's idolatry, he didn't plan on setting Baal worship between God and the children of Israel.

He just wanted to tack it on, so to speak, because the power and sensuality of Jezebel appealed to him.

A few years later, though, Elijah could truthfully say, *"I alone am left a prophet of the* L*ORD;* [who was willing to stand up and be recognized] *but Baal's prophets are four hundred and fifty men"* (1 Kings 18:22).

I am sure it was the same with the abusive Roman Catholic priests. They did not intend to lead their followers completely away from God—they only wanted to use their authority as a bit of "leverage" to procure some personal satisfaction.

Seeking affirmation apart from God can be dangerous.

I believe this ploy worked better than they had intended because when an already impressionable young person goes to an adult of religious authority, it's easy for the child to be manipulated into thinking salvation and forgiveness can come only through that leader.

In short, these priests replaced God in the minds of the young people they abused. They made themselves idols and consequently taught idolatry to children.

Although I'm sure it was never phrased this way, the children learned that enduring abuse was an act of worship; it was their service to God, the only way they could be sure to earn the priests' favor and, by extension, the favor of God.

Before the sexual abuse, there was an abuse of authority.

Children have a natural desire to please those in authority, and they are inclined to believe that those placed over them have their best interests at heart.

This is also a characteristic of wounded and vulnerable adults. For example, a woman driven to guilt and shame for her sins is easily manipulated by a leader who convinces her that he holds the key to her forgiveness.

Some women can attest, in fact, to having been lured into ungodly relationships with leaders during a state of vulnerability while they were seeking spiritual guidance.

Instead of being pointed in the right direction—toward Christ—they were given a shoulder to cry on and a warm embrace that led to years of involvement that they thought were impossible to break, no matter how they tried.

Anyone with a wounded heart, an inferiority complex, or a guilty conscience can be vulnerable to a mind-set that looks to a pastor or leader for affirmation instead of to God.

Abusers make a practice of fueling this fear and self-doubt with even more uncertainty so that their victims depend more and more on them.

Once the authority figure has replaced God as an affirmation-giver, it takes little time for him to replace God in other areas as well.

Sometimes abusers provide affirmation by placing a person with a wounded spirit and low self-esteem in a position of authority and then convincing that individual that he or she would never have been a success without the leader's help.

Basically, an abusive leader will do anything to foster dependence on himself.

For the victim, the process is something like walking down a gently sloping but extremely slippery hillside. The victim might not even notice she is going downhill; and even if she does, she may not be able to get back up again—every step sends her slipping further down.

The subtle process of abuse is also somewhat like being anesthetized for surgery. A good anesthesiologist doesn't strap your mask on, turn around, and flip on a torrent of sleeping gas.

Instead, she adjusts your mask, asks if you're comfortable, and continues making small talk.

Many patients don't even notice when her hand slips back to turn on a trickle of gas, and most don't remember at what point they fall asleep.

Abuser and victim may both be blind to the abuse.

Similarly, in authority abuse, the victim never sees it happening—and sometimes the authority figure doesn't, either!

Sadly, though, the abuse of authority is often a deliberate, selfish exercise of manipulation by a person whose own imbalanced and ungodly emotional needs demand that other people look up to him.

I once heard the story of a young man so bent on pleasing his earthly leader that he became convinced that he couldn't look to the True Master—God—and that God couldn't look at him if his human spiritual leader was not pleased.

This flies directly in the face of God's Word. Remember what Jesus taught? There can be only one master:

> *No man can serve two masters: for either he will hate the one, and love the other; or else he will hold to the one, and despise the other.* (Matthew 6:24 KJV)

Jesus applied this truth to the pursuit of money, so we usually think of it in that context.

It is, however, a principle that can be applied throughout all of life, and the message is clear: you cannot serve God—*the* Master—while simultaneously showing more loyalty to another master (such as mankind).

We must be wary, because leaders inside and outside the church often use tactics of fear, shame, and guilt to control and manipulate their followers.

Remember, though, that any time a man's voice is stronger than God's voice, it stunts spiritual growth, opens the door to other sins, causes division in marriages, and even destroys entire families.

Whenever a leader deceives people into thinking *he* is the only way for them to receive or hear from God, he has begun abusing his authority. That deception places him in a position that only God is supposed to occupy—and the Lord is less than pleased with that.

Remember what He said in Exodus 20:5: *"For I, the LORD your God, am a jealous God."*

He will not share His glory. As a pastor, I would never dare to become one of the wolves, leading His sheep away by competing for His position as *the* Shepherd.

> I know of an instance in which a man (I'll call him Thomas) began seeking God's guidance about owning a home. God answered his prayers by beginning to prosper his business and opening the door for the man to buy an affordable home for his family.
>
> Seeing that all these things had been taken care of, one of his friends asked Thomas, "Well, what are waiting for? God has opened the door and answered your prayers. When are you going to move in?"
>
> "Well," Thomas replied, "I need to take it to the authority first."
>
> Realizing that Thomas's idea of authority was the pastor (not God), his friend responded, "But you've been praying, and God has answered your prayers by giving you the finances and the home to purchase. What will you do if the 'authority' tells you not to purchase a home for your family?"
>
> "Well," Thomas answered, "I guess I'd just give that dream up, because if God is really leading me in this direction, then He will let my leader know as well."

This was truly a pastor in a position where he did not belong—his power put another man on the verge of self-destruction and tempted the wrath of God.

Christ died so that men and women could come directly to Him, and while we should maintain *respect* for those in authority over us, we should not use them as our *rites of passage* to hear from God.

Christ alone is our High Priest. (See Hebrews 4:14–15.) His death and resurrection have already paved the path to the Father. He even left us the road map with directions to get there: the Word of God.

Nowhere does the Bible say a Christian's life should be micromanaged by the earthly spiritual authority over him. Instead, it gives guidelines for living a godly life—including guidelines for taking responsibility of decisions God has given each individual.

These individual decisions are not for a pastor to decide unless the Christian simply cannot understand what the Bible says on the subject.

Even then, it is the pastor's responsibility to lead the seeker through the Word toward the answer—not to give him commands.

Have You Been Taught to Fear Your Leader?

I vividly remember my childhood prayer—"Dear God, please don't let the pastor find out that I sinned"—and I know for a fact that my pastor wasn't the only leader to control his people with fear.

This sense of fear, an indicator of abuse, is most noticeable in conservative, "old-school" ministries. Usually the minister begins with good intentions, trying to mold his parishioners into stellar Christians.

Far too often, though, I've seen it degenerate to a point where the leader, showing a lack of Christlike character, uses people's weaknesses against them.

Remember, his responsibility is to nurture and protect the people God has placed in his church. Thundering self-righteous judgment from the pulpit is neither Christlike nor edifying, and controlling people through emotional blackmail is sinful. A pastor should be both firm and compassionate, never too eager to learn about other people's faults. After all, it's not news that we all sin.

> *Again, the gift of God is not like the result of the one man's sin: The judgment followed one sin and brought condemnation, but the gift followed many trespasses and brought justification. For if, by the trespass of the one man, death reigned through that one man, how much more will those who receive God's abundant provision of grace and of the gift of righteousness reign in life through the one man, Jesus Christ.*
>
> (Romans 5:16–17 NIV)

One person (Adam) is responsible for all sin; one Person (Jesus) is responsible for all righteousness. We live with the sin nature that originated in one person's disobedience.

> Control through emotional blackmail is sinful.

When Adam, the first representative of our race, made his decision to sin, all humanity turned away from God and our nature became bent toward evil.

As Romans 5 says, however, Jesus came as a second Adam, who was *"a type of Him who was to come"* (Romans 5:14). Jesus was another God-chosen representative for the human race. He gave us the opportunity to turn back to God.

So the Gospel is not a message of condemnation as some abusive leaders would have us think but rather a message of freedom and empowerment. We should be able to rejoice—not roll in worry, shame, guilt, and fear—because although we received death sentences, Jesus carried our sin to the cross to make forgiveness and eternal life available.

Unfortunately, though, we in the body of Christ have become so hypocritical that if a person who sincerely loves God commits a sin that becomes publicly known, we mark the individual. We talk about him, we avoid him, we hold him up as a moral lesson.

Every time a pastor is tempted to do this, he should ask himself, "What if God marked me every time I committed a sin? What if He made an example of me?"

Instead of restoring our sisters and brothers, we've sought to control them by holding them hostage in their weaknesses: "Don't forget, I know you have this problem; don't go too far and don't rub me the wrong way or I'll expose you."

Spiritual blackmail is a terrible testimony for the body of Christ. When a sister or brother is overtaken by sin, we, spiritual ones, to restore that individual to Christ, not through name-calling and self-righteous finger-pointing but through the love and guidance of Christ.

Never think you're too spiritual to be tempted.

We must remember that although we ourselves may not be actively engaged in sinful acts at the time, we're all prone to become enticed by and engage in certain sinful activities when the opportunity presents itself. Thinking you're too spiritual to be tempted by anything is the greatest weapon Satan could use to ensnare you with your own deceit.

God is so faithful to His people that He has never showed me someone else's mess unless he or she was set in sinful ways to the point of desiring sin over holy living.

Even then, it was only when their sin was hurting the rest of the church that God spoke to me.

Otherwise, it's none of my business. I like to help my people if I can, but I refuse to take God's authority over sin into my own hands.

Remember, it is *God* whom we are to fear:

> *Let us hear the conclusion of the whole matter: Fear* ***God*** *and keep His commandments, for this is man's all. For God will bring every work into judgment, including every secret thing, whether good or evil.*
>
> (Ecclesiastes 12:13–14, emphasis added)

Has Your Immediate Authority Been Overridden?

We cringe when we hear about leaders who become too involved in the day-to-day activities of marriages and families. I think usually we're just reacting under a certain "gross-out" factor; it's unpleasant for most people to think about a third person having a say in their personal lives.

This kind of abuse, though, is actually more serious than gross. When a leader begins dictating policies for households that are not his own, he starts doing something the Lord never approves of: overriding the God-ordained order of authority.

And it came to pass after these things that Naboth the Jezreelite had a vineyard which was in Jezreel, next to the palace of Ahab king of Samaria. So Ahab spoke to Naboth, saying, "Give me your vineyard, that I may have it for a vegetable garden, because it is near, next to my house; and for it I will give you a vineyard better than it. Or, if it seems good to you, I will give you its worth in money." But Naboth said to Ahab, "The LORD forbid that I should give the inheritance of my fathers to you!" So Ahab went into his house sullen and displeased because of the word which Naboth the Jezreelite had spoken to him; for he had said, "I will not give you the inheritance of my fathers." And he lay down on his bed, and turned away his face, and would eat no food. But Jezebel his wife came to him, and said to him, "Why is your spirit so sullen that you eat no food?" He said to her, "Because I spoke to Naboth the Jezreelite, and said to him, 'Give me your vineyard for money; or else, if it pleases you, I will give you another vineyard for it.' And he answered, 'I will not give you my vineyard.'" Then Jezebel his wife said to him, "You now exercise authority over Israel! Arise, eat food, and let your heart be cheerful; I will give you the vineyard of Naboth the Jezreelite." (1 Kings 21:1–7)

Remember that when God first gave the land of Canaan to the Israelites, He told them,

The land must not be sold permanently, because the land is mine and you are but aliens and my tenants. Throughout the country that you hold as a possession, you must provide for the redemption of the land.

(Leviticus 25:23–24 NIV)

First Kings isn't clear about whether Ahab intended to buy the vineyard permanently and thus break the law God had established.

Do not revere a man more than God.

Even if Ahab was willing to obey the law, though, Naboth had the right to turn him down. Being steward of a family heritage was a serious thing, and the decision to accept or reject Ahab's offer was given to Naboth by the Lord Himself.

So, despite the fact that Ahab had offered a very fair bargain, Naboth was not unreasonable in holding onto his vineyard—he was just being conservative.

Ahab recognized the rightness of Naboth's decision, and while his reaction—sulking like a spoiled child—was not godly, his thinking certainly was: he accepted the fact that God had given Naboth immediate authority over the vineyard even though he himself had authority over Naboth.

Jezebel, however, recognized no such thing. She said to Ahab, in effect, "Some king you are! Stop being such a baby! I'll get the vineyard if you don't have the stomach for it."

She arranged to have Naboth murdered and then gave the ownerless vineyard to Ahab. It seemed legitimate because there was a kangaroo-court trial before Naboth was "executed," and it was also perfectly legal for a king to take over stewardship of land if the immediate owner passed away.

But God was not fooled. He sent the prophet Elijah to tell Ahab, *"Because you have sold yourself to do evil in the sight of the* LORD*...I will bring calamity on you"* (1 Kings 21:20–21).

Notice that the judgment didn't come just because Ahab agreed to murder. Rather, it was because Ahab, under the influence of the Jezebel spirit, *"sold* [himself] *to do evil."* That evil was overriding and warping the structure of authority God had set in place, and for this there would be punishment.

You see, the order of authority means so much to God that Jesus Himself never violated it. As a child, Jesus submitted to His parents even when they didn't understand who He was or what He meant when He explained His calling. (See Luke 2:41–51.)

In fact, the first time he was recognized as the Lamb of God, Jesus was *submitting* Himself to the work of God accomplished by the baptism ministry of John.

When Jesus came to the river Jordan to be baptized, John didn't want to do it. He said, in effect, "I can't baptize You! This doesn't make any sense. I need You to baptize me!"

Jesus Himself never violated authority.

John had a point, too; he was "only" a great prophet, while Jesus was the very Son of God!

But Jesus insisted. After all, how could God be righteous if He didn't play by His own rules?

The Father was using John to call people to repentance and commitment. It was impossible that the Son be too proud to participate. Jesus, as a leader, followed the chain of authority God had established for that point in time.

Now, imagine what it would have been like if Jesus had shown up at the Jordan, tossed His robe aside, and called out, "Okay, I'm here! I'm the real authority. God sent me straight from heaven. John's been baptizing you in the water of repentance, but I am the living water. Form a line; I'll get you really straightened out. Hey, John! Come on over. You can be first. I love you—you know you've done a great job, so don't be prideful now! God will bless you if you submit to His authority, you know."

God could not be righteous if He didn't play by His own rules.

This is what happens when leaders try to run households that are not their own. They trample the God-given ministries of husbands and fathers just as surely as Jesus would have been trampling John's ministry of baptism.

When abusive leaders disrupt the natural flow of growth and maturity in households, they cause stable homes to collapse and already weak families to crumble. Troubled homes are easy prey for authority abusers.

Even in cases in which the home appears stable, though, the abuser may try to step in, usually subduing the man of the house first, because it's impossible to really control a household without the man's consent.

Sometimes the leader will convince the man to surrender control under the guise of "supporting the leadership."

Other times he will simply undermine the man by cultivating influential relationships with the wife and children until the man becomes a stranger in his own home.

Regardless of how it happens, it's not "tough love"; it's manipulation, a trademark of the Jezebel spirit.

Anyone Can Check In; Nobody Checks Out

I remember preaching during a three-night revival at a church where, on the surface, everything looked wonderful. The praise and worship was wonderful, and the church was clean.

The building could accommodate about fifteen hundred people, but I noticed on the first night that only about 150 people had attended the service. I wondered why.

By the second night, I noticed the pastor's wife had a very controlling attitude. A large number of members in the congregation did not like her, but they fell under her authority.

That same night, I was invited to the pastor's house for dinner—a dinner served by several people from the church. They were not working as waiters and waitresses but in the form of household servants. They were spoken to harshly, belittled, and chastised for not giving their "services" to the "man and woman of God" for free. They were constantly told that this was "why they were cursed."

I had noticed that these people did not have a car but were using the church van to get around. They were living in the guest house, cleaning the church and the pastor's house, and meeting many of the needs of the ministry.

They were giving their lives wholeheartedly to the ministry, compensated solely by their living quarters in the guest house and the few groceries the pastor and his wife would purchase for them.

By the third night, I couldn't take it anymore. I confronted the pastor and his wife to talk to them about how they were treating these people.

They explained to me that these people had been "sent to them by God" because they were such "lowlifes," adding that God was using the ministry to bring them up to a level where they could be accepted by society.

I asked, "Don't you think they should be compensated on an individual basis, taught how to own a car and home, and become educated and empowered to move forth?"

The pastor's response was the Lord had told him that giving money to this type of people would hurt them. He said, "They'd never be able to excel; that's why God sent these particular people to our ministry."

This ministry had taken an obvious turn toward cultish behavior. During the three nights I was at this church, several people in the congregation whispered to me and asked if they could come to North Carolina to sit under our ministry at Bethel Family Worship Center.

They also told me that they were afraid, though, because they had been told they'd be cursed if they ever left the church or the ministry. Ultimately, they remained where they were because they did not want to be cursed.

The church is in a terrible state when the saints of God are more afraid to leave the church than they are to leave God.

Today, people remain in churches for years—drying up, receiving no refreshment from the quenching Word of God, because the teaching of "obedience" has been perverted and shoved down their throats to the point where idolatry becomes an acceptable practice—all in the name of Lord!

Leaving God is a curse in itself.

You see, to be led by the Spirit, you must spend time in God's Word. Sadly, though, the average Christian only reads the Word of God when he or she comes to church. Therefore, people will believe whatever is preached because they don't read the Word of God for themselves.

As in the case above, many people are frequently fed the lie that leaving a church will result in their being cursed. You don't get cursed by leaving churches; leaving *God,* however, is a curse in itself.

You cannot properly serve God while simultaneously doubting His Word and remaining in a situation that is not His will.

Only the grace of God can keep us, and it's this grace that should guide us in our actions. You simply can't live under the condemnation, "If you leave this church, you're gonna be cursed." That is blatant, ugly authority abuse.

A "curse" doesn't have any power unless people believe the lies and accept whatever wicked things are spoken. In other words, even if I were to speak evil over someone, I would just be making noise *unless the listener received and believed the words I said.*

The curse mentality can be debilitating.

No pastor can curse you, no matter how much you "dishonor" his authority.

You are the only one who can curse yourself, and this is based entirely on how you think. It's your thinking that will curse you and your thinking that will block you.

One of the worst curses that can happen is for you to be ignorant of who God wants you to be, accepting lies from a leader and staying in a situation that is not God's will.

This curse mentality—the notion that things are going wrong in one's life because of "disobedience"—can be debilitating. If we could only break past this barrier in the body of Christ, we could get great victory for everybody.

I learned a long time ago that it doesn't matter if you tell me, "You're just no good." You see, that's only your opinion; I'm living under grace, and, through Christ, I'm just fine.

I've heard people say things like, "The reason I can't meet my bills and stuff like that is because I'm cursed."

Do you know what I found out about the people who can't pay their bills? Do you know what the real curse is? Believe it or not, it's not the fact that they don't tithe. Many people fail to tithe, and their bills are still paid!

Don't get me wrong; I believe tithing is a scriptural way to give God our best. But do you know what the real curse is?

It's a refusal to sit down, look at your expenses, and make a budget that you can commit to.

If you make a specific, honest plan for how you need to spend your money, I guarantee you'll find that you have a bit more than you actually need!

That sounds more complicated than it really is. Many people don't think they could stick to a budget, so instead of trying, they shrug their shoulders and say, "Well, maybe I'm cursed."

You need to get your eyes off of other people. Stop focusing on what other people have and what they're doing.

"Well, everybody's getting a new car except for me, and I just feel so cursed." If your car works, drive it! And remember, you don't know about your neighbor's problems with his new car or all the credit bills and overdue payments he has to deal with.

> Grace means appreciating what you already have.

Obey the rule Grandma used at dessert time: "Don't look at anybody else's plate."

Don't allow yourself to follow someone else and mess up what God has going for you.

True grace is recognizing and appreciating what you have in your hands instead of trying to keep up with everybody else's "prosperity."

No pastor can take grace and contentment away from you, even if you leave his church, for these gifts are grounded in a relationship with Jesus Christ.

If you keep God first and don't allow another authority figure into that place, you can never be cursed.

Here's one last thought about any authority figure who claims to be a servant of God but threatens people with curses:

> *With the tongue we praise our Lord and Father, and with it we curse men, who have been made in God's likeness. Out of the same mouth come praise and cursing. My brothers, this should not be. Can both fresh water and salt water flow from the same spring? My brothers, can a fig tree bear olives, or a grapevine bear figs? Neither can a salt spring produce fresh water. Who is wise and understanding among you? Let him show it by his good life, by deeds done in the humility that comes from wisdom.*
>
> (James 3:9–13 NIV)

Can You Disagree with the Leadership?

As the previous section showed, going against an authority figure who harbors a Jezebel spirit can be a terrible thing. Consider Naboth: Ahab had him killed.

An abusive leader can force you out of your place in the ministry, business, or home; ruin your good name; or (less blatantly) destroy your confidence in who God wants you to be.

I have seen situations in which the abused parties were afraid to confront the abuser about his actions because "questioning the man of God" released a torrent of correction designed to pound them back into line.

People have been suspended from worship teams, banned from prayer meetings, and set down for hours-long "talks" with leaders who spend the whole time discussing the supposed attitude of the person who dares to question his leaders.

> A young man named Jacob went to his senior pastor about some fairly serious issues. Because Jacob was the youth pastor, he was responsible for raising money for the youth group to take trips and do activities. Jacob had a knack for raising funds, and the youth could bring in more money with a fund-raiser than the senior pastor drew from a typical Sunday morning missions offering.
>
> About a year before their "talk," the pastor asked if the youth would consider donating some of the proceeds from their fund-raiser to boost the church's missionary giving—a favorite project of the senior pastor. Jacob presented the request to the youth group, and the teens decided to sacrifice one of their scheduled trips in order to help the missions program.
>
> A few months later, the pastor asked again for help, but this time he told Jacob to announce the decision to the youth instead of making a request. The kids weren't to be consulted, he said, about how the ministry should be run; they should learn to submit to the authorities in the church.

> As time went on, things progressed to the point where no one but the senior pastor knew the total income from youth fund-raisers because no one was allowed to touch the money before he had taken out the portion allocated for missions.
>
> The money that remained for the youth program was hardly sufficient to keep it afloat, and Jacob faced criticism from church members for not doing enough with the teens. The kids stopped coming out for fund-raisers, too, because they knew they weren't going to see the fruit of their labor.
>
> Jacob tried to explain this to the senior pastor, who merely leaned back in his chair, stared at the ceiling, and drummed with his fingers as Jacob poured out his heart.
>
> As soon as Jacob finished, the pastor leaned forward in his chair, pointed his finger, and said sternly, "Well, what's clear to me is that we have some attitude issues to discuss."

This was a classic case of authority abuse. Jacob's pastor refused to take responsibility for his actions and wouldn't let anyone question his decisions.

In an effort to bring Jacob back into docile submission, the senior pastor "apologized" at the end of his rebuke. "Now, I want you to know that I'm really sorry that you've felt this way about things. I understand why you might have taken things this way, and I'm sorry. You know that I want what's best for you and the kids, and you just need to trust me, okay?"

Sadly, Jacob stayed under this abusive influence for another year and a half while the youth group dwindled down to a handful of cynical teens whose parents insisted they attend.

It was then that the church board learned the pastor had stooped to actually embezzling church funds for his personal use. He was asked to resign, and Jacob also left in search of a fresh start.

The Diagnosis

These guidelines should be used carefully when you are trying to determine whether you are in an abusive situation. Remember, the Jezebel spirit is deceptive, and the abuse of authority can be subtle.

Also remember, though, that your own perceptions can be clouded by frustration or disappointment.

If you are afraid to approach your pastor about an offense, seek God to know why. Is it because you are naturally shy? Because you're not sure that you're right? Or do you fear retribution of some kind?

That's just an example of how you must examine your heart; the issue goes deep and is not simple. I trust, though, that these guidelines will enable you to see the Jezebel spirit wherever and whenever it is at work.

When you find it, consecrate yourself to God and let Him lead you into restoration. Later we will talk in much greater depth about restoration.

First, though, I want to examine the most common kinds of authority abuse.

6

PASTORAL PARASITES

Did I commit sin in humbling myself that you might be exalted, because I preached the gospel of God to you free of charge?
2 Corinthians 11:7

A grievous type of abuse occurs in churches throughout America. Consider this example as we begin to discuss authority abuse committed by pastors and church leaders.

A church in North Carolina began as a powerful ministry for developing and preparing ministers. They moved into a small area and, in a matter of about two years, they'd grown from approximately thirty members to about 150.

It wasn't long before they were able to move from their first building into a much nicer one, and they just kept growing from there. God blessed them abundantly, to the point where they began equating material things with His favor on their lives.

Soon they began swaying toward a "Naming and Claiming It," "Get Rich Quick," and "Everyone Should Be a Millionaire" mentality. Over time, the daily diet of that ministry became a "prosperity gospel."

Around the fourth or fifth year of the ministry, the prosperity teachings grew into badgering the congregation for failing to attend every service and for having sinners as friends. The leaders began teaching a practice of "cutting off" family members who did not go to their church and even went so far as to reprimand families for going on vacations and celebrating holidays (Christmas and Easter included), insisting that families should instead bring money spent on those occasions to the church.

Eventually, marriages inside the church began to decay. The ministry's total focus had become television and bullhorn preaching, and there was no spiritual food provided for families.

These family breakdowns marked the passing of the last spiritual breath in that church. The appearance of life continued, but no healthy fruit could grow on the ministry's "branches," stunted by abuse.

It may not be obvious at first, but a lot of today's teachings on prosperity and blessing have taken on a strong flavor of the Jezebel spirit.

One thing you will notice if you read the accounts of Jezebel in 1 and 2 Kings and Revelation is that she is always self-serving. She pumped a lot of money and effort into the worship of Baal—but only because she believed it would increase her favor with the gods. She spent money and manipulated the government to increase her husband Ahab's power base—but only because it increased her own power at the same time.

In the same way, I believe you won't find a man preaching a prosperity gospel unless it enhances his life in some way. For some such pastors, it is simply the adoration they get from congregations of people who love hearing about God's "fail-proof plan to prosper you."

Poverty is not a penalty for sin.

For others, it is the prestige of leading an ostensibly opulent, wealthy church.

And still for others, it's God's money slipping into their own pockets, put there by a carefully arranged kick-back system.

Regardless of their motives, the gist of these messages is the same: that we should look prosperous and act prosperous even though our income may not permit us to carry out a lifestyle of prosperity.

You might be surprised by the popularity of this ungodly teaching that everyone in the body of Christ should be a millionaire. Often, this kind of teaching implies that those who do not have wealth are somehow sinning against God! What a tragic lie.

No wonder many in the body of Christ have confused the word "prosperity" with "debt." I've received many letters through the years from people complaining that they practiced the prosperity principles taught to them only to find their homes now suffering from overwhelming debt accumulated as they aimed at becoming "prosperous."

I define *prosperity debt* as spending beyond your means to present the illusion of a prosperous life that does not exist.

Webster's Collegiate Dictionary defines *prosperity* as "the condition of being successful or thriving; economic well-being."

How can an individual thrive or enjoy the benefits of economic well-being if, drowning in debt, he pursues an image that doesn't exist?

This evil teaching has caused the body of Christ to believe that the "just shall live by debt" instead of by faith. Many people invest money in fine clothes, for instance, successfully looking the part but always lacking bare necessities, such as furniture and food, because they are consumed with bills.

Live by faith, not by debt.

It's tragic when a spiritual authority saddles people with this prosperity lie instead of teaching them about true riches and helping them escape a worldly value system.

Many churches in America refuse to allow people to pass their new members' classes unless they have an annual salary of at least $25,000 or $30,000. Their theory is that allowing poorer people into the church will offset the general prosperity and diminish the "blessing of God." In many churches, if you're not part of the elite group of people who earn astronomical sums of money, you're shunned or ostracized.

This behavior contradicts what the apostle James taught about wealth:

> *My brothers, as believers in our glorious Lord Jesus Christ, don't show favoritism. Suppose a man comes into your meeting wearing a gold ring and fine clothes, and a poor man in shabby clothes also comes in. If you show special attention to the man wearing fine clothes and say, "Here's a good seat for you," but say to the poor man, "You stand there" or "Sit on the floor by my feet," have you not discriminated among yourselves and become judges with evil thoughts? Listen, my dear brothers: has not God chosen those who are poor in the eyes of the world to be rich in faith and to inherit the kingdom he promised those who love him? But you have insulted the poor...If you really keep the royal law found in Scripture, "Love your neighbor as yourself," you are doing right. But if you show favoritism, you sin.*
>
> (James 2:1–9 NIV)

People who work two or three jobs and are unable to devote time to God because they become engulfed with debt or the pursuit of cash are running after another god, whose name is mammon (money). *"Ye cannot serve God and mammon"* (Matthew 6:24 KJV).

Pastors who teach people to focus their lives on pursuing wealth are teaching them to worship a false god.

You must understand that it is the will of God that all His children be blessed and in health. God truly is concerned about prospering both our soul and our finances. It is the will of God that we all pay our taxes, enjoy a vacation, and have savings.

But these things are supposed to be small parts of a God-centered life; the notion that they should be central or the idea that God's plan requires outright wealth is a perversion of truth and a clear instance of authority abuse. How does it benefit someone to look prosperous but lack the means to ever enjoy *authentic* prosperity?

Breaking Out of Prosperity Debt

A mind-set of prosperity debt is really a poverty mentality in disguise. You see, poverty is a way of thinking, and until your mentality changes, your lifestyle won't, either.

Unless you confront the lie of prosperity debt, it will eventually wipe you out.

Most of us have enough money to meet our needs but lack the discipline to manage funds properly. The Word of the Lord says that if you're faithful over a few things, He'll make you ruler over many. So why would He place you in a seventeen-bedroom mansion when you can't pay $2000 each month in rent?

I've spoken with people whose monthly rent was $12 per month because they were on the government-funded program called Section Eight—and yet their rent payment was still several months overdue. If you cannot manage $300, then a million dollars is never going to come your way.

To break out of the poverty mind-set, first make a budget for yourself. Having this kind of commitment will help you resist the pressure to spend money you don't have.

List your income and expenditures; if your expenditures exceed your income, start immediate spending cuts. Make sacrifices and eliminate those things you do not absolutely need—things like dining out, cable television, recreational shopping, going to the movies.

Instead, cook dinner at home, borrow a movie from a friend, or read a book. Cook a large, simple dinner at the beginning and middle of each week and become fond of leftovers until your income exceeds your expenditures.

It's important also that you identify your genuine needs. Do you really *need* another sweater—or golf club, or television—or do you merely *want* one?

God will supply all of your *needs* according to His riches in glory (see Philippians 4:19).

Unfortunately, though, people have been taught to lie about God when it comes to obtaining things that make them feel good. They say God told them to purchase this or that, even when their purchases cause them to plummet into the abyss of debt. Converting *wants* into *needs* is a spiritually dangerous practice.

Converting wants into needs is a spiritually dangerous practice.

Think before you buy. I once saw a pair of patent leather shoes in Chicago that I knew my wife would like, so I bought them. When I went to New York, I saw the same shoes and bought them again, not realizing I'd already purchased them in Chicago. At home, I found yet another pair of the same shoes already in my wife's closet. I'd bought the same pair of shoes on three separate occasions!

This could have been avoided if I had thought through each purchase instead of buying the shoes impulsively. This time, failing to count the cost made a funny story to tell on myself, but a *lifestyle* of compulsive buying steals food from the table to buy grown-ups' toys and trades necessities for trinkets.

Many people have made serious mistakes because they were greedy and didn't know how to be satisfied and content. You must ignore teachings about the lie of prosperity debt—a downward spiral of materialism and debt is not the best God has for you!

He wants more for you than living one paycheck away from being homeless. No one who tells you otherwise truly cares for your well-being.

> Wealth is not sinful as long as we do not pursue it before God.

The Word of God does not say that we can't be wealthy or have cash; it only says we cannot allow the pursuit of money to become a priority over serving God.

A story in Matthew 26 teaches an important lesson on this: in our lives, the Lord is always to take precedence over money.

In this story, a woman approached Jesus with an alabaster jar of spikenard. Spikenard was an extremely valuable spice, usually mixed with the purest olive oil.

Since investing in a business was unheard of in those days, people put their savings into valuable things that could be stored safely, such as gems and precious metals. People who could not afford jewelry often invested in spices, especially spikenard.

So when this woman unexpectedly broke open the jar and poured the contents over Jesus' head, she was probably emptying her life's savings. She gave Him the only thing of value that she'd salvaged from her sordid lifestyle; in a sense, she offered her whole life to Him in this single act.

The disciples didn't see it this way, though. They were offended and indignant! *"To what purpose is this waste?"* they demanded (Matthew 26:8 KJV). She could have sold the spice and given the profit to the poor, they argued.

It was Judas, the group's treasurer, who was the most upset. As he watched the oil soak into Jesus' robe and puddle on the dusty floor, no doubt he envisioned all that money evaporating into thin air.

The disciples placed their love for money above the love the woman had for Jesus—but she refused to hold material possessions as more sacred than God.

> *But when Jesus was aware of it, He said to them, "Why do you trouble the woman? For she has done a good work for Me. For you have the poor with you always, but Me you do not have always."* (Matthew 26:10–11)

"Sowing" into Abuse

Some pastors continually preach prosperity and become prosperous, while the majority of their congregation remains impoverished.

I will be blunt: when an authority figure demands constant giving without giving anything back to those under him, he is guilty of abuse.

Any time you hear a gospel that works for only a select few, you should be suspicious, because God is no respecter of persons. (See Acts 10:34.)

The truth is that those pastors usually get rich not because they get up every morning to go to work but because they take what the congregation gives them.

Such leaders use God as bait in their con-artist scams by saying, "Do this for me free of charge; allow the Lord to use you." They teach that the way to become prosperous is to give, give, give—and they never teach principles of responsibility, saving, and godly discipline.

There are some churches in which the pastor is so greedy that he continually pressures and badgers the congregation to give more—while he continues to take and use more for himself, pastoring from a storefront church with his fine car parked outside the door.

Giving is good when paired with responsible saving and discipline.

I pastored my church at Bethel Family Worship Center for five years without a salary, but my family was always taken care of; our needs were always met. Why? Because we did not depend on the congregation to meet our daily needs. I owned businesses and gave out of my own pocket to build and renovate a house for God first.

My only goal was—and still is—to minister the Word of God and to teach people to give cheerfully of their time, talent, and finances while improving their own lives in the process.

This is not to say that I am against pastors receiving a salary; on the contrary, I think they should receive compensation for their services. But because I obeyed the principles the Lord showed me by first building Him a house, my businesses have flourished and the church has grown at an amazing rate.

> You will reap what you sow.

The Bible says that you reap what you sow. (See 2 Corinthians 9:6.) Those who sow large amounts into their beauticians have wonderful hair but little else.

Those who sow large amounts into their wardrobe have wonderful clothes but could drown in credit card bills.

Those who sow large amounts into an abusive authority will reap nothing but spiritual abuse.

> *The rain comes down, and the snow from heaven, and do not return there, but water the earth, and make it bring forth and bud, that it may give seed to the sower and bread to the eater.* (Isaiah 55:10)

Too many Christians have been caught in the trap of spiritual gambling. They believe that if they give all they have, God will return the "favor" with abundance.

Treating Jesus as a pair of dice, the saints of God have been taught to cast a throw, cross their fingers, and chant, "Come on, Jesus!" while waiting for a return.

We're told to "live by faith" while simultaneously being taught to sow our bread and to eat our seed. This is a huge trap.

For instance, your rent or mortgage payments, utility bill, car note, child-care costs, grocery bill, and other household expenses are your "breads."

Tithes, offerings of thanksgiving, special pledges, charitable giving, and random acts of kindness are your "seeds."

Taking care of our own needs is part of God's will.

Teaching people to give all that they have is not biblical. When God gives you money, He expects you to do a number of things with it, and believe it or not, any person who gives all of his money to the church is outside of the will of God. Some of our money is to be reserved for "bread;" taking care of our own needs is part of God's will.

"As the rain gives seed to the sower" means seed is given for us to plant in the ministry; likewise, *"bread to the eater"* means the remainder of our income is to be disbursed within the home to meet our daily needs.

Some people give to the church money that should be allotted for bills and upkeep of the home; this explains why the money they give never yields a harvest.

You do not have to give your rent money to the church to receive a blessing from God. You must never sow bread in the hope of reaping a tree that brings forth fruit, for only seed can do that.

When you offer your bread up to God instead of your seed, God is not pleased with your sacrifice. An authority who tells you otherwise is abusive—plain and simple.

Today, I'm very careful about where I sow seeds. Some people have determined in their heart never to change; to sow into them or their ministries will only further their stubborn will and their aggression against others.

> *Do not give what is holy to the dogs; nor cast your pearls before swine, lest they trample them under their feet, and turn and tear you in pieces.* (Matthew 7:6)

Do not cast your pearls to swine and do not feed the children's bread to dogs. Those who are selfish do not know how to cherish spiritual gifts—which is why they pressure men to give to them rather than seeking God first in times of crisis.

Those who are givers, however, know how to get God's attention in the midst of crises.

> *In those days Hezekiah was sick and near death. And Isaiah the prophet, the son of Amoz, went to him and said to him, "Thus says the LORD: 'Set your house in order, for you shall die, and not live.'" Then he turned his face toward the wall, and prayed to the LORD, saying, "Remember now, O LORD, I pray, how I have walked before You in truth and with a loyal heart, and have done what was good in Your sight." And Hezekiah wept bitterly. And it happened, before Isaiah had gone out into the middle court, that the word of the LORD came to him, saying, "Return and tell Hezekiah the leader of My people, 'Thus says the LORD, the God of David your father: "I have heard your prayer, I have seen your tears; surely I will heal you. On the third day you shall go up to the house of the LORD. And I will add to your days fifteen years."'"* (2 Kings 20:1–6)

King Hezekiah was sentenced to death by God, but since he had obeyed the Lord's commands, he could turn his face to the wall and put God in remembrance of His Word: *"Remember now, O Lord, I pray, how I have walked before You in truth and with a loyal heart, and have done what was good in Your sight."*

God responded by reversing the verdict: *"I have heard your prayer, I have seen your tears; surely I will heal you."*

Those who give of themselves with a pure heart and with the purest intentions know how to get God's attention. Because they give willingly and from a cheerful heart, God opens up the windows of heaven and pours out profuse blessings on them.

After the guest speaker had finished speaking one night during our annual tent revival, people started lining up to give their offerings to the Lord. Sensing some were giving out of an emotional response and not because God had spoken to them, I approached them. "Is this your last?" I asked each one.

> Giving from a pure heart gets God's attention.

I instructed those who replied affirmatively to put their money back in their pockets, have a seat, and enjoy the rest of the service.

Some sacrifices are necessary and biblically correct, but timing will always reveal God's will when such sacrifices are necessary. Deuteronomy 15:11 says, *"For the poor will never cease from the land; therefore I command you, saying, 'You shall open your hand wide to your brother, to your poor and your needy, in your land.'"*

The principle behind this verse is why many rich, successful people—even those who don't know God—give to charities: they understand the law of reciprocity.

When you do sow seed, make sure your motives are pure. You should not sow solely to receive.

God will equip us to be a blessing to others.

Instead, sowing must be an issue of the heart—full of compassion, ready to deal alms to the poor, and out of your lack into the life of one whose needs are greater than yours.

Ask yourself, "For whom have I done something nice lately without expecting anything in return?"

When we obey God's principles for giving seed, He promises to bless us according to our need. As a result, we become better equipped to be blessings for others.

God wants to bless us in such a way that we can be released corporately to touch one another's lives.

The bottom line is that you should give according to what the Lord has blessed you with and give as He has commanded you to give.

If you're a teacher, teach for the Lord; if you're a painter, paint a room in someone's house for free; if your closet is filled with shoes, find someone whose shoes are falling apart and bless him with your best pair.

It is every Christian's responsibility to learn how to handle money and gain respect for it. Tell yourself you are the head and not the tail; then, take the necessary steps to make that statement true: spend wisely, give God what belongs to Him, help meet the needs of others, and take care of your own household. *"For wisdom is a defense as money is a defense"* (Ecclesiastes 7:12).

If you want to feel a sense of security, refuse to bow to an abusive authority. Turn to God, exercise godly wisdom, and save some of your income. Tell yourself this is the year that you will make drastic changes in your economy; break free from the bondage of materialism. And *"if the Son makes you free, you shall be free indeed"* (John 8:36).

7

RELIGIOUS HOME-WRECKERS

Beware of false prophets, who come to you in sheep's clothing, but inwardly they are ravenous wolves.
Matthew 7:15

Authority abuse happens in churches, but it can come a lot closer. It can enter our homes.

Kathy and David were like many American couples. She attended church regularly, while he preferred going only occasionally; he never prevented his wife from pursuing her spiritual growth, though.

Kathy, in her enthusiasm over finding a new church, eventually convinced David to come along one Sunday. He immediately noticed major caution signs that warranted his concern, but his wife and children had already fallen under the spell of the pastor's manipulation. They were so completely engrossed in this church that David felt helpless to deliver them out of it.

He watched as his wife began running the household as if he were merely her roommate; instead of consulting him, she sought guidance solely from the church pastor and allowed him to influence every aspect of life.

"Why is this man my wife's security?" David wanted to know. "And what is my position in the home now that this other man has become the strongest voice of influence over my family?"

In his effort to avoid fanning the flames of disagreement and to keep peace with his wife and children, David began compromising the structure of his own home for what the leader felt was best for his family.

While the pastor increased his influence as the virtual leader of their home, David became increasingly helpless and hopeless as his voice was silenced and his power was paralyzed. The cataclysm of this collapse came during a birthday celebration for his daughter, Allison.

Allison had always been a daring and ambitious teenager, and for her sixteenth birthday, she wanted to celebrate by bungee jumping from a tall pinnacle.

David adamantly refused to allow this and made it clear to his daughter and the entire family that until Allison became an adult—until she was old enough to make her own decisions—he would in no way support or allow such a dangerous stunt.

To David's surprise, however, the church pastor made an announcement in front of Allison and all her peers that he had purchased a bungee cord and secured the area for her to take her birthday "leap of faith," despite the disapproval of Allison's father.

Neither the pastor nor David's wife had shared this information with David before the announcement; they knew how strongly David opposed it.

Now, the secret was out. Allison was overwhelmed with enthusiasm, and David sat on the sideline, watching helplessly as his family slipped away from him and into the hands of the man who'd taken up spiritual residence in his house without his permission.

David was forced to watch his teenage daughter climb to a high pinnacle, then plunge headfirst toward the earth.

Fortunately, the jump was a success. Allison was fine, but her enthusiasm at having succeeded in what her father had feared only strengthened the bond between the children, David's wife, and the pastor. All David could do was retreat into himself and wonder, *How did this happen to my family?*

For an abusive pastor or leader to move into a home, there must be room for him. Unfortunately, this pastor had all the room he could ever want.

Although he meant no harm, David did leave a spiritual vacuum in his home. By failing to make his own relationship with God a priority, he forfeited the spiritual authority God wanted him to exercise in his home.

Even though his wife and children were visibly interested in growing after God, David was not. His attitude said, "You go ahead if you want to," and this left his family looking for someone else to follow.

They found that leader in the abusive pastor—and you already know the rest of the story.

Who Is My Husband?

Ron was an overachiever. He wasn't especially talented or even much smarter than the average guy—he'd tell you that right off. But he was determined; he'd been taught all his life that doing things right and working hard were all he needed to be a success.

He never stepped on anybody else. In fact, sometimes he'd help coworkers up a rung on the ladder of success and then double his own efforts in order to pass them again.

He tithed ten percent of his income, attended church twice a week, and gave five percent of every other paycheck to help fund missions.

He worked ten to fifteen hours of overtime each week and spent his Saturdays fixing up the house, maintaining the lawn for his wife, Nina, and coaching Little League baseball.

Every morning before he left for work, he and Nina would read a Psalm and pray together. Friday night was "date night," and Ron never took his cell phone along.

To top it off, he visited a stress-management specialist once a month to make sure that he wasn't developing any self-destructive habits.

There was only one problem. *"I feel like I'm Ron's second job,"* Nina wrote in her journal. *"I know he loves me – at least, I'm pretty sure he does. But he never asks me how I'm doing or compliments me unless we're scheduled to have time together. I can count on him to take good care of me, but I'm only one part of his life; I don't think he really wants to share the whole thing with me. I feel like I don't really know who he is. I don't know the same man that his coworkers see or that his Little League kids know. They tell me he's wonderful, and the man I see is wonderful, but it's not the same person. Why won't he let me in close?"*

Nina worked part time at the church because she and Ron had agreed not to have children for the first seven years of marriage, and this position provided her with a healthy way to use her strong organizational and interpersonal skills.

Nina was good at her job, and her employer, the associate pastor, made sure she was properly recognized.

After a while, he went further, occasionally complimenting her on her appearance and randomly stopping by her office to thank her just for doing her job. Basically, he began giving her the kind of extra attention Ron didn't seem to know she needed.

Over time, and without her really knowing how it happened, Nina found she cared more for the pastor's approval than she did for Ron's. She bought clothes that pleased the pastor's taste because she knew he would notice, and she began consulting him before she made decisions.

Despite Ron's best efforts, a vacuum remained in Nina's life—a vacuum the abusive pastor used to increase his own status. The marriage began to crumble, and a bewildered Ron worked desperately but futilely to salvage his perfect life.

Now, don't think for a moment that I'm excusing these abusive pastors. What I am saying is that, by leaving room for the abusive authority to take over, these two husbands—David and Ron—failed to protect their families.

Families must not leave room for abuse to enter.

A true shepherd, on the other hand, would have worked to help David and Ron become godly men who could truly lead their households. What happened to their families was evil and sprang from the self-promoting wickedness of abusive leadership.

Often, leaders like this won't even wait for a "hole" to open up in the families under them. If there is no place for them to work, they'll set out to make one.

We established that authority abusers need the people under them. Because they need others to help them, they will go to great lengths to keep a family under their influence.

Worst of all is when an authority abuser deliberately sets out to win the heart of a family member. An abusive pastor won the heart of David's wife by fulfilling the spiritual needs David could not. He won the heart of David's daughter by giving her more of what she wanted—in this case, personal freedom—than her father thought wise.

In every case, an abuser will seek to one-up the rest of the family in order to win over his target. He might buy his secretary the car her husband couldn't afford, even if her husband just purchased her second-choice car. He might give a young man a place on the worship team, even though the young man's parents feel his time should be devoted to education.

It takes a strong marriage and a strong family to stand up under the attack of an abuser who determines to drain their life like the juice from a battery.

Making a Hole

If a family is healthy and able to withstand an abuser's influence, the abuser's first step is often to twist the teaching that a person's first love belongs to God. (See Revelation 2:4.) These teachers almost always brush aside what the Bible says in the book of Matthew about a man and his wife becoming one flesh:

> *And He answered and said to them, "Have you not read that He who made them at the beginning 'made them male and female,' and said, 'For this reason a man shall leave his*

father and mother and be joined to his wife, and the two shall become one flesh'? So then, they are no longer two but one flesh. Therefore what God has joined together, let not man separate." (Matthew 19:4–6)

God used the term *"one flesh"* to describe what happens when two people leave their own agendas and influences to live entirely within the marriage.

> Divided houses are easier to control.

They need to sacrifice their personal objectives whenever necessary in order to minister to each other. Their focus is on the vision God has for them—the vision they should share as if they were the same person.

Teachers with a Jezebel spirit usually argue that this joining is merely physical, though, and that a married couple remains two people in spirit.

They may cite Revelation 2:4, which refers to God as our *"first love,"* to support this belief.

I've even heard pastors teach that before God presented Eve to Adam, He first *"knew"* her—both physically and spiritually—Himself! There is no scriptural evidence to support the idea that God did any such thing.

The real reason that the Jezebel spirit wants to separate spouses is because it makes them easier to control. Haven't we all heard the phrase, "Divide and conquer"?

Yet somehow these false teachers make it sound very plausible. "If you really love God more than anything else, you will follow Him (and do what I say) no matter what anyone thinks, even your spouse," they say.

What angers me is that this teaching completely ignores God's righteousness! How could a righteous God break His own laws? If He said it is sinful to dissolve a marriage, how could He rightfully break one up?

It's no good to say He is God, and to misuse Scripture—"His ways are higher than our ways"—to justify unbiblical practices. The Bible does say that God is higher than we, that His righteousness is purer than ours. (See Isaiah 55:9).

But to say that His righteous plans could be something totally different from what He has already expressed is ridiculous. His righteousness is the standard that we are to use to determine our own plans!

Do not listen if leaders misuse Scripture to justify unbiblical practices.

This one lie opens the door to a giant crypt full of ghastly things. First, this false separation creates the possibility that God would call one spouse in one direction and the other spouse in another direction. (Some churches actually advocate divorce as "God's will" for situations such as this.)

This lie almost guarantees that the authority abuser will be able to hold on to at least part of a family.

You see, after having drilled this evil, icy wedge between marriage partners, the abuser doesn't really have to worry if the man of the house becomes suspicious or righteously indignant about the abuser's actions.

The husband might even decide to leave the abusive church, but his wife won't go with him. If the abuser has convinced her that God wants her to stay, she will leave her husband and cleave to the ministry—a perversion of Jesus' command.

This kind of situation actually helps the authority abuser more than a healthy family does! A man or woman who has abandoned his or her spouse for an abusive ministry will be extra needy and have something to prove. A wife will pour herself out, supporting the abusive leader in ways no healthy individual would.

Playing the role of an adviser and protector, the abuser gets to soak up all her love and attention at no cost to himself.

Another thing this false separation between husband and wife creates is the possibility that one partner is more "spiritual" than the other. If the abusive leader cannot convince his victim that God is purposely separating her from her husband "for the kingdom's sake," he may begin telling her that her husband is simply walking away from God.

Often, the abuser will seem very compassionate. He will tell her, "Your husband has such a calling of God on his life, such an anointing! He could be a world-changer, an absolute dynamo for God! I love his spirit...but...if only he didn't have such trouble submitting to authority."

A steady diet of this kind of talk will eventually convince a woman that her husband has a rebellious heart and is wasting his God-given talents. By the time he leaves the abusive ministry, she may be ready to divorce him.

Again, this plays right into the abuser's hands; for every gifted man he loses, the abuser gains the fanatical devotion of an equally gifted woman (or vice versa).

It doesn't help that most churches today have an activity or two going on every single night of the week. Not that I'm against activities; I think it's good and healthy for people to get together during the week to minister and fellowship with each other.

The problem is when an abusive authority starts making people feel guilty for missing even one meeting during the week.

Abusive churches break families apart.

When this happens, families begin to disintegrate. Couples don't spend time together because they are organizing and attending their own special programs.

Kids and teenagers don't spend time with their parents because they're packed off somewhere with their peer group and a youth pastor.

An abusive church completely replaces the family—and we wonder why families break down!

Even worse, abusive ministries infiltrate the family, separating husbands from wives and children from parents. A husband has no time to be advised by his wife, and he has no opportunity to teach her what God is teaching him, according to Paul's instructions:

> *Husbands, love your wives, even as Christ also loved the church, and gave himself for it; that he might sanctify and cleanse it with the washing of water by the word.*
>
> (Ephesians 5:25–26)

There is no opportunity for children to learn from any adults except the abuser's hand-picked "spiritual leaders."

A whole generation can grow up under an authority abuser and never be equipped to know that something is wrong!

Stand Up!

In chapter five, we examined how the Jezebel spirit loves to override the God-given order of authority. When King Ahab wanted to make inroads on Naboth's family inheritance, Naboth stood as a godly man should and refused to let it happen.

But Jezebel was at work in Ahab's life, and she provided the deception and "muscle" to override Naboth's authority. The only way Naboth could have escaped her was to have somehow transported his vineyard out of Israel, away from her influence.

Confront abusive leaders and give them the chance to change.

Obviously, he couldn't cart a piece of real estate around with him.

But the inheritance that God has given you is not in land; as Paul said, *"The kingdom of God is not eating and drinking, but righteousness and peace and joy in the Holy Spirit"* (Romans 14:17).

In other words, God's kingdom is not about tangible assets—it's about the hearts and souls of his people. Because this is true, you can protect your inheritance.

Matthew 18:15–17 gives us guidelines about what to do when someone sins against us. If you have recognized your leader's behavior as abusive, you are responsible to confront him and give him the chance to change. Jesus said that, *"If he hears you, you have gained your brother"* (v. 15).

But if you follow all of God's instructions for communicating with the abuser and he still refuses to change his ways, Jesus said, *"Let him be to you like a heathen and a tax collector"* (v. 17).

In other words, pack up your vineyard and get out of Jezebel's reach! Don't stay where an authority abuser can pick at the walls of your inheritance and hammer at the foundation of your family.

Get out from under the abusive ministry and away from the satanic influence. Abuse is never God's will for your family, and He has given the head of every household the authority to prevent it.

8

Domestic Dictatorships

All of you be of one mind, having compassion for one another; love as brothers, be tenderhearted, be courteous; not returning evil for evil or reviling for reviling, but on the contrary blessing, knowing that you were called to this, that you may inherit a blessing.
1 Peter 3:8–9

Sometimes the abuse of authority enters our homes not from without, but from within.

The platoon of Marines was clustered in a small grove of trees. Just across the field lay an enemy stronghold. Nobody knew how many people were inside. They couldn't even be sure they remained unnoticed as they sneaked down the hillside to where they now were.

Stan Jones took a step backward, bumping into Smith, who banged the back of Jones's helmet with his fist.

"Watch where you're going, stupid!" Smith yelled.

"Hey, you were in my way!"

"Now look, you two," John raised a hand in warning. "Knock it off. We need to get across that field and into the trees as quietly as we can."

"No, you look," Smith growled. "You're not in charge. Kravitz was, and he's not here now. We rank as high as you, and I say that this looks like a minefield. We need to flank them."

"Kravitz left me in charge, Smith," John spoke icily. "Stand down, or I'll knock you down."

"Try it," Smith challenged.

John did. Smith fell. Smith got back up, and this time John fell. In an instant the entire group of men was a melee of swinging fists and boots. They were so preoccupied with the fight that they didn't even notice the shadowy figures surrounding them until machine-gun fire cut them all down.

Seems ridiculous, doesn't it? No one would be foolish enough to indulge in a petty power struggle that close to a deadly enemy, would they? Sadly, I see this kind of foolishness almost every day in marriages. *"Marriage is honorable among all,"* according to Hebrews 13:4.

Where is the honor, though, when so many marriages are ending in divorce? Although the two are supposed to become one, they often remain separate entities, fighting for the throne of power through manipulation and control.

This struggle is a sad abuse of the quest for authority. Husbands seek to control wives and wives seek to manipulate husbands, while the enemy seeks to destroy them both.

Often, couples are so preoccupied with their own struggles that they fail to see that the fallen world is trying to tear them apart.

> There's more to marriage than "I do."

Many marriages that God created to annihilate the enemy have found themselves under enemy fire, possessing the weapons to defeat that enemy but lacking the readiness to draw those weapons in defense.

The battle becomes most tragic when one half of the couple begins abusing his or her God-given authority over the other or over the entire family.

In the book I wrote with my wife Jeannie, *Crazy House, Sane House,* my wife discusses many of the challenges we experienced early in our marriage.

We married as soon as she graduated from high school and found out the hard way that there's more to marriage than simply, "I do."

I had grown up with an abusive and dogmatic father, but it wasn't until after my wife and I got married that these same tendencies began surfacing in me and I started acting out my father's abusive habits with my wife as my target.

Screaming at one another or simply not speaking at all constituted our communications while I sought to control my wife with my domineering personality.

I refused to respond when she tried to communicate her concerns, and eventually she began to shut down as well.

Though we lived in the same house, we became two separate entities. Our children even began looking at me as "the strange man in mommy's house."

The "silent treatment" exacerbates problems.

Using the "silent treatment" instead of simply telling your partner your needs is a dangerous game to play.

Although most people only resort to the silent treatment when all else fails and communication has produced no results, it's still a product of deceit that only exacerbates the problem and complicates the situation.

Early in my marriage, I would simply shut down whenever my wife did not like the way things were going. My attitude said, "I'm the man of the house, and that settles it!"

This dominating way of handling our problems left no room for communication. Because my wife had no way to process her feelings and no outlet for expression, she began yelling to release her emotions.

With a smug look, I'd simply look at her and ask, "What are you yelling about?"

I made her feel guilty for refusing to see things my way. We were definitely in a war with one another. The outcome of such shut-downs is not resolution but bitterness. Many women today are bitter because certain men accept only a one-sided view of every situation and refuse to communicate, thus treating their wives with apathy and negligence.

As I began relinquishing my "throne" of control, we were met by one more challenge. Because I traveled a lot and was often away from home, my wife and children had formed a special bond; they had their own way of doing things.

Consequently, I was often like a guest or stranger in my home. Whenever I looked in the refrigerator, for instance, my children would run to my wife and say, "Mama, *he's* in the refrigerator," as if I were a guest and not the father of the home.

My wife would have to explain that it was okay for Daddy to get something from the refrigerator.

Once I began spending more time at home, my children relaxed and welcomed my presence, and we enjoyed spending time together.

> Marriage is two partners committed to one another's future.

Because my wife had created her own environment to deal with my absence and the emotions she'd started to suppress, it was initially difficult for her to relinquish her control in our relationship.

Her thoughts were, *If I let go, he's going to win, and I want God to punish him for what he's done to me.*

She explains, though, that as I became more active in the home and relinquished my "control," and after we began working together as a team, releasing her control became an honor instead of a task.

Because we both wanted desperately for our marriage to work, we each stepped aside and allowed the other to contribute to the marriage instead of focusing on who was going to "win" the next battle.

So many homes are in trouble today because one spouse wants to lead, and the other refuses to follow bad leadership.

Marriage, though, is not to be a system for ungodly control and manipulation; it is to be a refuge for support and encouragement.

Though marriage will experience challenges—and so it should—it is a place for unification where both parties must be committed to securing the fulfillment and growth of one another's future, enjoying the fruits of two who have truly become one along the way.

"Thank God I'm Not a Woman"

Sadly, it seems the church has done more than any other institution in history to demean women.

In the fourteenth century, poet Geoffrey Chaucer wrote what became the oldest surviving work of fiction ever written in the English language—*The Canterbury Tales.*

In one of his tales, a woman from the city of Bath complains at great length about the typical attitude of religion toward women.

It seems that in her day, religious leaders wrote entire books trying to convince people that women could not be trusted and should be kept under tight rein by their husbands.

The Wife of Bath complains that her husband wouldn't even buy her nice clothing because he thought it would encourage her sinful imagination!

This suspicious, dominant male behavior is a far cry from the way Jesus Himself treated women while He was on earth.

Jesus treated women with respect.

Hebrew society at that time was so man-centered that, at every synagogue service, the Hebrew men prayed, "Blessed art thou, O Lord, who hast not made me a woman."

Yet when a woman who had been a prostitute anointed Jesus with oil and washed his feet with tears of repentance, Jesus defended her actions, telling critics,

> *Assuredly, I say to you, wherever this gospel is preached in the whole world, what this woman has done will also be told as a memorial to her.* (Matthew 26:13)

In another instance, a woman with an unstoppable hemorrhage broke several Old Testament laws while seeking healing.

She sneaked through a crowd of people and actually touched Jesus, even though she was ceremonially unclean and should have been stoned for her audacity.

Because of her faith, though, she was healed immediately. Jesus—who was on His way to heal the daughter of an important man—stopped everything to make the woman "'fess up" in front of the whole crowd.

He didn't do this to punish her, though; when she identified herself, Jesus said tenderly, *"Daughter, be of good cheer; your faith has made you well. Go in peace"* (Luke 8:48).

I'm hardly the first person to point this out, but it bears repeating, too: when Jesus rose from the dead, He didn't immediately show Himself to any of "the boys"—not even to John the beloved!

Instead, He appeared to a lady whose love for Him kept her at His tomb after the disciples had left.

> *But Mary stood outside by the tomb weeping, and as she wept she stooped down and looked into the tomb. And she saw two angels in white sitting, one at the head and the other at the feet, where the body of Jesus had lain....Now... she turned around and saw Jesus standing there, and did not know that it was Jesus. Jesus said to her, "Woman, why are you weeping? Whom are you seeking?" She, supposing Him to be the gardener, said to Him, "Sir, if You have carried Him away, tell me where You have laid Him, and I will take Him away." Jesus said to her, "Mary!" She turned and said to Him, "Rabboni!" (which is to say, Teacher). Jesus said to her, "Do not cling to Me, for I have not yet ascended to My Father; but go to My brethren and say to them, 'I am ascending to My Father and your Father, and to My God and your God.'"* (John 20:11–17)

It's clear that Jesus respected and honored women.

During His day, one of the most popular Bible scholars taught that a man could divorce his wife if she upset him for any reason—including burning his dinner!

Jesus disagreed with this idea:

The Pharisees also came to Him, testing Him, and saying to Him, "Is it lawful for a man to divorce his wife for just any reason?" And He answered and said to them, "Have you not read that He who made them at the beginning 'made them male and female,' and said, 'For this reason a man shall leave his father and mother and be joined to his wife, and the two shall become one flesh'? So then, they are no longer two but one flesh. Therefore what God has joined together, let not man separate." They said to Him, "Why then did Moses command to give a certificate of divorce, and to put her away?" He said to them, "Moses, because of the hardness of your hearts, permitted you to divorce your wives, but from the beginning it was not so. And I say to you, whoever divorces his wife, except for sexual immorality, and marries another, commits adultery." (Matthew 19:3–9)

An open-minded reading of the four Gospel accounts will clearly show that Jesus treated women with a level of respect and gentleness unusual for the time.

Why, then, have His followers been so infamous for their poor treatment of women?

The Jezebel spirit takes every chance to promote itself, especially when someone else will end up in a more easily controlled position. But I think that this poor treatment of women has a lot to do with a misunderstanding, too. For a lot of people, "Submit to authority" means the same thing as, "Be a doormat."

Family Authority

Wives, submit to your own husbands, as to the Lord. For the husband is head of the wife, as also Christ is head of the

> *church; and He is the Savior of the body. Therefore, just as the church is subject to Christ, so let the wives be to their own husbands in everything.* (Ephesians 5:22–24)

Let's go back to the purpose of godly authority: *to nurture and cultivate whatever is placed under it.* This definition doesn't allow for a wife to be a doormat while her husband is a set of heavy boots.

Look at the rest of the apostle Paul's instructions:

> *Husbands, love your wives, just as Christ also loved the church and gave Himself for her, that He might sanctify and cleanse her with the washing of water by the word, that He might present her to Himself a glorious church, not having spot or wrinkle or any such thing, but that she should be holy and without blemish.* (vv. 25–27)

Husbands are to love their wives just as Christ loved the church. And how did Christ love the church? He gave Himself for her. Well, that's simple enough. A husband is to be willing to die for his wife if he has to.

But wait—is that what "giving your life" always means? Is that how you gave your life to Christ?

Of course not. You're still alive and breathing as you sit there and read this book. You're very much alive; but your life isn't your own, is it?

If you sincerely committed yourself to Christ, you gave Him permission to inconvenience you. You promised to give your life to Him, moment by moment.

You see, Paul wasn't talking about a husband giving his life for his wife in some heroic, snap-decision moment; he said God demands the much harder sacrifice: day-by-day, moment-by-moment sacrificial love:

> *Love is patient, love is kind. It does not envy, it does not boast, it is not proud. It is not rude, it is not self-seeking, it is not easily angered, it keeps no record of wrongs.*
> (1 Corinthians 13:4–5 NIV)

And Paul wasn't finished! He wrote,

> *So husbands ought to love their own wives as their own bodies; he who loves his wife loves himself. For no one ever hated his own flesh, but nourishes and cherishes it, just as the Lord does the church.* (Ephesians 5:28–29)

This is how a healthy marriage is to function.

I told the following story in *Crazy House, Sane House,* to illustrate how much fun it can be to bless your wife's development:

> Some time ago I asked my wife, "What do you want to do with your life?" I encouraged her to set goals and to pursue them. She has many gifts, and it is up to me to encourage her to develop them.
>
> A few weeks later, she came to me and said, "I want to go back to school." I was pleased with her decision.
>
> Now my wife has an accounting business in which she handles millions of dollars, manages properties, makes sure the bills are paid on time, does payroll, pays insurance, and all kinds of things.

> It is not enough for me just to acknowledge Jeannie; I must invest in her life. I feel free to invest in her because I feel secure in my own position before God. I have reaped the benefits of my investment countless times.

I have found that the more I encourage Jeannie to grow and the more I build her confidence in the gifts God has given her, the stronger our marriage becomes.

Marriage can make authority abuse hard to recognize.

And as she becomes a more capable person, I become a more capable minister! Her growth really is my growth because we are dedicated to the same vision.

Back when I was "king of my household," I was stressed out and always on the run. It was too much for one person to handle!

From where we are now, it is easy to see how badly I was crippling myself by depriving Jeannie of the opportunities and encouragement she needed.

No man who wants to keep his wife "in her place" has any idea how much joy and strength he could find by letting her stretch her wings!

"[Love] *always protects, always trusts, always hopes, always perseveres*" (1 Corinthians 13:7 NIV).

Enter the Dictator

We've already talked about how subtle authority abuse can be in the context of the church. Let me emphasize that the abuse of authority can be more deceitful and more difficult to recognize in marriage than in any other relationship or institution.

This is mostly because marriage is such an intense relationship; the opportunity is that much greater for a man's sinful nature to make a mess of things.

Most people think an abusive husband is an alcoholic or a drug addict. When they envision abusive husbands, they think of raised voices and the sounds of shattering glass and screams echoing through the walls late at night.

Trust me, that does happen far too often. Anyone who can think clearly about physical abuse knows that the woman should get out of the relationship.

There are many forms of marital abuse, though, that don't look nearly as ugly as physical abuse—yet they do just as much damage to a woman's spirit.

When a man deprives his wife of fellowship, approval, and physical affection in order to starve her into submission, he is disobeying his mandate to love and cultivate her. I call this *the abuse of neglect*, and such behavior constitutes rebellion against the very reasons God gave the man authority over his wife.

Physical abuse isn't necessarily the ugliest.

I have described some of the effects my own icy stranglehold had on Jeannie, and I know that her heart was severely damaged. I feel my past behavior gives me the right to be forceful on this subject, since I speak passionately from a humble heart that learned its lesson the hard way.

My wife has forgiven me, and, thanks to God's incredible grace, there is no lasting scar on her heart or our relationship.

The fact remains, though, that for a time I abused the authority I had over her—I was an abusive husband, although I doubt anyone around us would have guessed it.

Many Christian men—abusive and otherwise—like to quote the apostle Paul to their wives. Here, Paul was talking about marriage and the responsibilities each partner has to the other:

> *The husband should fulfill his marital duty to his wife, and likewise the wife to her husband. The wife's body does not belong to her alone but also to her husband. In the same way, the husband's body does not belong to him alone but also to his wife. Do no deprive each other except by mutual consent and for a time, so that you may devote yourselves to prayer.* (1 Corinthians 7:3–5 NIV)

You can probably imagine how many husbands have used this passage while trying to wring more sexual intimacy out of their wives.

I could say a lot about the proper usage of this passage, but right now I just want to reverse the usual spin people take on it.

You can pick up any book, newspaper, or magazine article about marital sex and find that all the experts, Christian and non-Christian alike, agree on one thing: enjoyment of sexual intimacy is almost completely physical for men and almost completely emotional for women.

There is nothing wrong with either side—this is how God designed things, and it works beautifully in a healthy marriage.

Let me phrase things a different way, though: for most women, the best part of sex happens before they ever reach the bed. The loving look in her husband's eye, the intimate conversations, and the act of sharing a life together are necessary ingredients for making a wife feel sexually fulfilled.

When a husband uses the abuse of neglect to get his way, he is shortchanging his wife.

There are other, more aggressive forms of abuse than the abuse of neglect. Because the controlling aspects of the Jezebel spirit always operate out of the same self-serving motivation, these forms of abuse look a lot like what we've discussed in previous chapters.

Does your husband insist your entire relationship with God be filtered through him? Are you afraid to make mistakes in front of him for fear he will make fun of you? Do you have to be extra careful to keep things "just so" in order to keep him from getting crabby? When you talk to him about his faults, does he get angry?

Many husbands don't know they are abusing authority.

Many husbands don't know they are abusing their authority. Selfishness doesn't look nearly so evil when it happens in the family den as it does when it crosses a pastor's desk.

Manipulation might not seem very ugly when it buys a husband a little extra time to work on his golf game, even though such manipulation in a church setting might be easier to identify as abuse.

As I've told you, it took both the Holy Spirit's work and my wife's steadfast determination to get through to me to help me see how I was abusing authority in my home.

Had my heart been much harder, I don't know if I could have seen how wrong I was. It was a hard lesson to accept, and changing my behavior was at first a bitter pill to swallow.

The spiritual influence and mental stance behind aggressive abuse starts with an often nonviolent struggle for control, and I don't want that fact to get lost in the graphic retelling of domestic horror stories.

Jesus never looked at the surface of things.

Remember, Jesus never looked at the surface of things; He dug deep to reach the root of the problem, plunging further until He reached the heart of the matter.

For example, when a young man asked Jesus how to get into the kingdom of heaven, Jesus didn't bring up any of the fellow's obvious shortcomings. The young man told Jesus he had kept the law of Moses ever since he was a child.

If I had been Jesus, I think I would have had something to say to this guy about lying! Nobody could or can keep the law of Moses without fail.

It was impossible for this young man or anyone to have kept it without fail. But Jesus zeroed in on the young man's biggest problem, the one thing he loved more than God: his money.

The absolute light of God's truth will illuminate the darkest closet as well as the corner behind the couch.

But it's the corner behind the couch that we often neglect, so that corner stays dirtier than many closets. Just as Jesus looked beneath surfaces, so too must we delve deep into the underlying causes of abuse.

9

Rebels and Rabble-Rousers

Therefore I exhort first of all that supplications, prayers, intercessions, and giving of thanks be made for all men, for kings and all who are in authority, that we may lead a quiet and peaceable life in all godliness and reverence.
1 Timothy 2:1–2

It wouldn't be fair to talk about leaders who abuse their authority over others without addressing followers who abuse the leaders in authority over them.

I don't intend to spend much time on the topic, though, because I don't think it's necessary. Over the years, leaders of all kinds have made strong cases for why they should have the respect and submission of the people under their authority.

But in order to promote a balanced view of authority, let's chat for a moment about rebels.

Remember our discussion of Lucifer's rebellion against God? Hundreds of years later, the prophet Isaiah, under influence of the Holy Spirit, mourned his fall:

> *How you are fallen from heaven, O Lucifer, son of the morning! How you are cut down to the ground, you who weakened the nations! For you have said in your heart: "I will ascend into heaven, I will exalt my throne above the stars of God; I will also sit on the mount of the congregation on the farthest sides of the north; I will ascend above the heights of the clouds, I will be like the Most High."*
>
> (Isaiah 14:12–14)

Notice the five claims this prideful archangel made. I call them the five "I wills": I will ascend into heaven, I will exalt my throne, I will sit on the mount, I will ascend above the clouds, and I will be like the Most High.

Authority is not based solely on talent.

When you boil these "I wills" down, you find that Lucifer simply couldn't stand the fact that God was greater than he was.

Perhaps we shouldn't be blamed for feeling the same way sometimes, right? After all, it's really a very democratic idea. No one should be better than anyone else. No one should tell anyone else what to do. People should talk about things and compromise, right?

Well, that makes for pretty good civil government. But that's not how God designed His kingdom to work, and that's not how the world in general operates.

Authority is not based solely on how talented an individual is, how qualified a person looks, or how available someone is to do a job no one else can do. Authority comes with position.

As Paul said, *"Let every soul be subject to the governing authorities. For there is no authority except from God, and the authorities that exist are appointed by God"* (Romans 13:1).

God gives authority as a gift of grace.

Aaron and Miriam, Moses' brother and sister, once got confused about this very point. *"So they said, 'Has the LORD indeed spoken only through Moses? Has He not spoken through us also?'"* (Numbers 12:2).

They were upset that Moses—whom they knew was imperfect—got so much authority over things when he wasn't the only person who had heard from God. They thought his authority came from his ability, and they felt they were as gifted as he was.

As God made very clear to them, though, Moses' authority was simply a gift of grace from Him: *"I speak with him face to face, even plainly, and not in dark sayings; and he sees the form of the LORD"* (Numbers 12:8).

God took Aaron and Miriam's rebellion so seriously that the cloud of His presence left the tabernacle, and he struck Miriam with leprosy until they repented.

I think it is important to notice *when* God dealt with Miriam's and Aaron's attitudes. He didn't wait until they had decided to ask for Moses' resignation; He called them on the carpet as soon as they began criticizing their leader.

I've told you that I go out of my way to be accessible to my people. Part of the reason for this is that I don't want them talking behind my back—for their sakes!

As the situation with Aaron and Miriam shows, God clearly doesn't take kindly to that kind of behavior. (Now, it's important to notice here that Moses didn't take matters into his own hands but let God take care of them. The account says, *"The man Moses was very humble, more than all men who were on the face of the earth"* [Numbers 12:3]. Moses let God handle authority issues of this sort.)

Sadly, criticizing leadership has become so commonplace that people joke about having "roast preacher" for Sunday dinner.

There are many reasons for such disrespectful treatment of authority, but they usually boil down to two motives.

1. Get Mad at God, Stone the Preacher

When the children of Israel left slavery in Egypt, the Lord led them toward the Red Sea.

Pharaoh, who was either unusually resilient or amazingly stupid, rethought his decision to let the Hebrews go. He had made his decision under the most extreme kinds of duress imaginable, and now concluded that he had been wrong to release the Hebrews from slavery.

So he gathered his best armored division (that's what chariots were in those days) and set out to recapture the Israelites.

When he found them, they were encamped by the Red Sea. On either side of them were steep, rocky cliffs.

The Israelites were terrified. It was like the end of an old Western movie, when the adversary has the hero trapped in a canyon. They could see directly ahead that they were boxed in on both sides. They had trusted God and fled Egypt, but it looked like God was going to hand them over to the Egyptians to be captured or killed. Understandably, they were quite upset!

> Many Christians get upset with God but blame the pastor.

Here is where they went wrong, though: instead of crying out to God, asking Him for an explanation and some help (as Moses did later), they turned against their earthly leader.

They accused Moses of deceiving them or, at the very least, of being a grossly incompetent leader whom they never should have trusted.

They decided that, since they were all going to die or be enslaved, they should execute Moses while they still had the chance. They would have stoned Moses had God not intervened.

I think a lot of Christians live in those moments before the parting of the Red Sea. So often when they become disappointed with God, they blame their feelings on the pastor.

If God does not heal them when they expect Him to, they accuse the pastor of preaching a lie.

If they tithe faithfully without getting the riches they expected in return, they demand that the pastor explain God's refusal to bless them.

And if they don't feel God's anointing in services as they think they should, they begin murmuring that the pastor must be an "old wineskin" who is quenching the Spirit.

2. I Could Do Better

A favorite of the Jezebel spirit is the idea that "I could do (*fill in the blank*) better than the person in authority is doing it."

Remember how Jezebel got the vineyard of Naboth for her husband? She usurped the king's authority by sending orders in Ahab's name, ordering that Naboth be executed on false charges. Her reasoning was that if Ahab couldn't get the job done, she'd do it for him.

This motivation is often at work in marriages and families as well as in churches. Almost everyone knows a man who is "whipped"—that is, completely submissive to his wife. She gets her way in almost everything and makes all the decisions. Do you think she would admit that she is controlling—or, worse, acting in the Jezebel spirit?

Of course not! I expect you could ask one hundred of these rebellious wives why they run their households, and every one would answer that it's because their husbands would do a terrible job if given the chance.

Now, it is true that abuse fosters abuse. When a woman has been hurt by a man, she will often vow never to let it happen again.

For most wounded women this means controlling every part of their own lives, including their husbands. Although this variation seems much more understandable, it still means the woman cannot or will not trust the authority God has put over her.

Once this idea gets planted in a person's head, it can be almost impossible to eradicate. I have seen an entire church staff at war with the pastor and with one another, all because a few people wanted the power to "do things right."

> We must submit to authority on earth and in heaven.

Jesus once told a story in which an estate manager refused to do anything with the money in his care because he believed his boss was cold-hearted and didn't handle profits correctly.

His three coworkers did their best to manage their responsibilities, and, at the business meeting, they were each awarded with a higher position in the company.

But the man who "knew better" than his boss was fired on the spot and fined for damages! (See Matthew 25:14–30; Luke 19:12–27.)

Jesus was saying—among other things—that no one who refuses to submit to authority will be trusted with responsibilities in the kingdom of heaven.

I have heard stories that would curl your hair—or straighten it out stiff if it's naturally curly. I was once told how the head intercessor of a neighboring church became convinced her pastor was not following God's plan for that church.

She began to pray that God would set him straight, but that is not all she did.

This woman, in her efforts to do better than the leadership was doing, began whispering in the ears of people on the worship team and of the associate ministers. She was highly respected and had a sincere love for the Lord, so people listened to her.

It was only a matter of months before it became obvious that the pastor was moving in one direction while most of the congregation and people in leadership were moving in another.

> Only God can break the cycle of authority abuse.

Before much time had passed, the board asked the senior pastor to resign and voted to replace him with the associate pastor.

The head intercessor had complete control over this man and was thus able to run the church. The former pastor left heartbroken, a victim of the sting of Jezebel.

The most frightening thing about stories like these is that they end with authority being passed on to someone who does not understand it at all.

When Jezebel installed Baal worship in Israel, she won indisputable victory by murdering every prophet of the Lord she could find.

I'm sure that in her mind, the ends justified the means. But as the murder of Naboth shows, she did not change once she had attained the power she wanted!

The same holds true for every abusive person who usurps authority. If someone uses manipulation and deceit to earn a place of influence, you can be sure that he or she will use manipulation and deceit to control the people under him or her.

In short, people who abuse the authority they are *under* will abuse the people they have authority *over*. The cycle of authority abuse will continue; and as we saw in the story of the Red Sea, only God has the power to break it.

10

Overcoming the Python Spirit

This chapter is designed to bring deliverance to those who find themselves in the death grip of authority abuse.

Reading and applying its message will cause you to walk in freedom from the suffocating spirit of authority abuse that squeezes the life out of its victims, consuming the remains of their collapsed and weary frames.

The attributes and behavior of this spirit is similar to an animal in the natural realm: the python snake. This reptile wraps itself around its prey and squeezes the life out of it to satisfy its appetite.

As we consider the essence of authority abuse and discuss the process of deliverance, it will be useful to think of this analogy in the natural realm. The python snake provides a fitting parallel that evokes the very first authority abuser: Satan.

Scriptural Precedent for the Serpent Analogy

From my studies, I know that in the book of Genesis, Satan took control of a serpent and used it as an instrument in his work of temptation.

He indwelled the serpent in the garden of Eden, where Adam and Eve lived in harmony. Satan's plan was to be the driving temptation to get Adam and Eve out of the garden, where they had been protected from all of the satanic devices that would be perpetrated and perpetuated by the human race.

God used Satan's evil schemes to redeem humankind.

Although Satan's plan intended to bring about humankind's utter demise, God used Satan's evil schemes to bring redemption to humankind. For we know that *"all things work together for good to them that love God, to them who are the called according to his purpose"* (Romans 8:28).

One of the questions that we may ask until Jesus returns is, Why did God operate that way? Why did He allow Adam and Eve to be tempted and subsequently evicted from the garden of Eden?

People have been asking this question for ages, and yet no one has received an answer—at least, no one has received an answer that we can authenticate as coming from God.

We think, *He could have just made us perfect,* yet are left wondering why He didn't. God is never without a plan or a purpose, however; His plan is for us to be perfect.

Now the God of peace, that brought again from the dead our Lord Jesus, that great shepherd of the sheep, through the blood of the everlasting covenant, Make you perfect in every good work to do his will, working in you that which is wellpleasing in his sight, through Jesus Christ; to whom be glory for ever and ever. Amen.

(Hebrews 13:20–21 KJV)

The serpent was Lucifer's agent to lure Adam and Eve into doing his will, which was to push them out of the garden of Eden.

Thus, God gave us His Son Jesus in order to restore us to Himself and make us perfect *"to do His will."*

Because we are dealing continually with this ever-present evil force, God allows us to go through a process in order to perfect His divine will within us.

The apostle Paul put it this way:

For I know that in me (that is, in my flesh,) dwelleth no good thing: for to will is present with me; but how to perform that which is good I find not. For the good that I would I do not: but the evil which I would not, that I do. Now if I do that I would not, it is no more I that do it, but sin that dwelleth in me. I find then a law, that, when I would do good, evil is present with me. For I delight in the law of God after the inward man: But I see another law in my members, warring against the law of my mind, and bringing me into captivity to the law of sin which is in my members. O wretched man that I am! who shall deliver me from the body of this death? I thank God through Jesus Christ our Lord. So then with the mind I myself serve the law of God; but with the flesh the law of sin. (Romans 7:18–25 KJV)

How the Python Spirit Operates

The reptile known as a *python* is "a large, non-venomous snake that crushes its prey." It kills its prey not by biting it or injecting venom but by squeezing, crushing, and suffocating it so it can swallow and digest it.

When I discuss the *python spirit,* I am not referring to a demon. Rather, I am referring to the spirit of individuals whose character and behavior—and the influence of these traits on other people—mimic those of a python in the wild.

> Authority abusers are inspired by the python spirit.

This type of spirit woos you into danger, becomes intimate with you, and finally kills you spiritually. It is the spirit that inspires all authority abusers.

When you are deceived by this false spirit, you begin telling yourself, "Nobody loves me like this person. This person makes me feel good about myself." But this person with a python spirit is forcing the life out of you. It is as if your spirit weighed 200 pounds but the python spirit has squeezed it down to 100 pounds in record time.

You may feel you're doing God's will seven days a week, but you are depriving your body of the spiritual nutrients necessary for a healthy, Christian life. Then, as you become spiritually incapacitated, the python suddenly begins sucking you in completely.

You can no longer think for yourself because you now live in the belly of a satanic spirit whose intention was always to consume you, thereby satisfying his greedy appetite.

He knew that he had to operate through deception, because if you had seen him as he truly was, you would have evaded him.

This spirit became your "friend" in order to inoculate your mind with its demonic agenda before drawing you in to crush you.

When an individual with the python spirit is finished with you, he leaves you spiritually crippled and in despair—you are actually lying in the belly of a predator.

This is a determined spirit that is not easily deterred. It is also completely confusing because it is a spirit that may attach itself to someone you love dearly or trust completely.

Often, this person is a pastor. We discussed in Chapter Six how pastors often abuse authority, but let's briefly revisit this issue as it relates to the python spirit.

Pastors Prey on Congregations

I come from a Seventh-day Adventist background. One of the blessings of being raised as an Adventist was our strong, scriptural diet.

In the Adventist church I attended in my youth, the teachers and ministers didn't just come up with ideas; their teachings were full of scriptural authenticity.

Today, I often hear preachers in the pulpit make up their own doctrine on the spot, attempting to justify it by saying something like, "This is the Greek definition."

When asked to substantiate their teachings, however, they come up short and cannot qualify their philosophies with biblical accuracy.

As a pastor, I have had to overturn erroneous teachings that former pastors instilled in the minds of gullible church members. Their understanding of the Word of God had been shaped by family traditions, religious rituals, and, yes, sometimes even doctrines of devils; challenging those beliefs sometimes caused offenses to arise.

No one is exempt from the python spirit's influence.

My job, however, is to continue preaching the truth, for with truth comes freedom (see John 8:32).

We all have an agenda, a purpose, and a point that we are trying to convey when we minister or speak to others. What better way is there to convince Christians of something (which may or may not be true) than to say, "God said"?

If an individual is using this method to prove a point, then what he or she says must be confirmed, qualified, or validated by scriptural truths before you allow a false idea to slither its way into your mind, and especially into your spirit.

An unfortunate thing about the python spirit is that none of us is exempt from its influence.

All too often, we act upon things that are drummed up from the enemy whose tendency is to add just enough truth to draw his victims close enough to squeeze the life out of them.

You must be able to move on without allowing the things you hear to ruin your life or cause it to stagnate. You must receive the Word of God and allow it to transform your life. The Word of the Lord is life, and it is powerful by itself.

> *For the word of God is quick, and powerful, and sharper than any twoedged sword, piercing even to the dividing asunder of soul and spirit, and of the joints and marrow, and is a discerner of the thoughts and intents of the heart.*
> (Hebrews 4:12 KJV)

The truth of God is not one-sided; it cuts in both directions. It is designed to cut off things that hinder your progress.

Soothsayers and Other Sources of Counsel

I often refer to the python spirit when ministering to individuals who tend to seek the counsel of soothsayers for spiritual guidance.

A *soothsayer* is "a person who foretells events," and *soothsaying* is "prophecy or prediction; a practice or art of foretelling events."

Although the word *prophecy* is mentioned in this definition, it does not mean biblical prophecy but foretelling of events by studying and interpreting the alignment of the stars, astrology, birthstones, dates, and other natural forces.

The sixteenth chapter of the book of Acts talks about a young girl who has the spirit of divination. Obviously, many people flocked to hear her direction; she *"brought her masters much gain by soothsaying"* (Acts 16:16 KJV).

Divination is "the act or art of foretelling the unknown; the practice of seeking to tell future events."

How does one practice foretelling events? Through stargazing, birthstones, crystal-gazing, or incense reading, a diviner practices until he or she learns the art.

Throughout the 1980s and 1990s, an overwhelming number of infomercials advertised psychics and their services. The popularity of psychics and psychic readings had waned, but today it is making a comeback; its credibility is increasing as well.

This next level of divination and sorcery that we are going to encounter is so powerful because it will encompass much truth with just a few lies attached. This means that you will find those who work the principles of satanic literature appearing to be blessed by their practices.

For example, the "law of attraction," which holds that individuals possess the power to draw to themselves what they believe and articulate, sounds similar to many of our scriptural teachings, such as:

> *For verily I say unto you, that whosoever shall say unto this mountain, Be thou removed, and be thou cast into the sea; and shall not doubt in his heart, but shall believe that those things which he saith shall come to pass; he shall have whatsoever he saith.* (Mark 11:23 KJV)

> *For with the heart man believeth unto righteousness; and with the mouth confession is made unto salvation.*
> (Romans 10:10 KJV)

But where does this teaching originate? Does it come from God, or does it come from bookshelves and mystical teachings?

It is the same brand of teaching, but something is horribly wrong.

It seems that more and more people are consulting mediums, psychics, therapists, or pastors for direction. Almost everyone is searching for enlightenment, understanding, a higher power, or a greater knowledge.

The python spirit is taking advantage of this trend, which brings to light the prophetic message found in Luke 10:2: *"The harvest truly is great, but the labourers are few."*

Psychics' predictions end with spiritual death.

There is a great harvest of individuals who desire a greater understanding of God, but the laborers are being corrupted by false doctrinal beliefs.

The python is lying in wait; he has us surrounded. But instead of rebuking him, we pet him as we would a harmless animal, thus promoting his demonic propaganda.

We are fascinated by the mystique of the pattern of his coat, blind to the fact that he is wrapping himself around our legs and preparing to pull us to our knees.

Soothsayers' practices and methods lead back to the python spirit. This practice or art of foretelling events by soothsayers is associated with a python because the predictions that you receive from soothsayers will ultimately end with spiritual death. (See, for example, Deuteronomy 18:14; Jeremiah 50:36; Micah 5:12.)

No matter how sweet, wonderful, or well-wishing a prediction may seem, it is earthly, sensual, and demonic (see James 3:15).

Although it may feel good to have your hand read by a palm reader, doing so opens the door to the *python spirit.*

You may get so caught up in wanting to know your future that you spend your fortune to find out your fortune. Charlatans will prey upon your vulnerabilities, promising to give you foresight about the future. In return, you will forfeit your enjoyment of the present.

This particular spirit preys on its victims by crushing and suffocating them after enticing them to learn about the unknown.

Many of us focus on the physical characteristics of individuals who make predictions, but our focus should be on the character of the spirit that is being used to deliver the message.

This spirit has to woo you, wrap itself around you, and squeeze you as if providing comfort. As it continues to tighten its grip, you realize that your life is actually being drained from you.

Gossip and the Python Spirit

The true essence of the python spirit can be summed up in one word: *gossip*.

Gossipers exhibit this same type of behavior. They fill their bellies with information regarding the lives of others, and when confronted, they will regurgitate all types of disgusting propaganda to save their own hides.

There is nothing so savory, delicious, and appetizing as a good piece of gossip—as long as it's not about you, of course. The Bible tells us, however, to avoid the sin of gossip. (See, for example, Proverbs 16:28, 20:19 NIV.)

Whether we admit it, all of us are prone to gossiping and likely to formulate opinions concerning others—especially today in the age of E-mail. At certain intervals, God has to come and whisper, "That's enough. Don't allow yourself to become caught up in those types of conversations."

Gossipers regurgitate disgusting propaganda.

When you start to deal with God, it's never about another person. It's God showing you yourself. You are not going to change the inherent pattern of the world; you can only make a difference, and the difference must start with you.

Ask yourself, *Why is it that when I fall, 'God knows my heart,' but when others fall, 'they should be ashamed of themselves'?*

If God's mercy can carry you through your trials, then it can surely carry others through theirs.

Deal, Don't Deny

After a python has swallowed its prey, it just lies there and waits for the digestion process to be completed.

Movement could mean death for the snake—the prey might penetrate its skin, stretched and weakened to allow passage of its prey.

Similarly, after it has killed something large, the python spirit just lies in silence. You can sense that something is amiss, however, because it appears to have grown strangely fat and complacent overnight.

When are real pythons caught, killed, and skinned for their skin to make beautiful shoes and bags?

When they have just consumed some of their prey, because this is when they are too fat and too delirious to move or defend themselves.

> When you determine to believe God, you will often come under attack.

They lie still as if everything is normal, but somewhere in the midst of all that is going on, truth and deliverance show up. Attack a python suddenly, and it will regurgitate its prey in order to escape and save its own life.

When we are dealing with the ever-present evil forces of the python spirit, we must make a decisive effort to do what is good rather than giving in to evil.

Why is it often easier to do what is wrong than to do what is right? Because we reside in a world where it seems as if evil is always present, and if you are not careful, your flesh will tend to adapt to the present-day environment.

When the desires and inclinations of your flesh war against your mind or your spirit, you must immediately cast down every thought that might attempt to squeeze the life out of you and exalt itself above the knowledge of God (see 2 Corinthians 10:5).

Often when you determine to believe God, you will come under attack.

Should this occur, you will have to deal with the attack; denying it will not cause it to go away. The more you make it out to be something that it is not, the longer it will take for you to be delivered from it.

We leaders in ministry are called to minister with a word to set the captives free, but is it possible for us to deliver and set people free from something from which we ourselves have not been set free or delivered?

The answer is, *Sometimes...but not in every instance.* The more time you spend in private communion with God, the more God will reveal to you your flaws and any idiosyncrasies from which you need deliverance.

This could explain why many people avoid spending private time with God: spending private time with Him is self-reflective.

When you avoid God, however, the scales of injustice become unequally balanced, favoring the side of evil. If you refuse to listen to God concerning your weaknesses, you do little to strengthen your defenses or even to become delivered from many of the frailties that are keeping you bound.

This bondage makes the perfect opportunity for the python spirit to find you in the darkness and prey upon your weakened state of mind.

My deliverance started more than a decade ago, before I began pastoring and preaching to others about being set free.

I am now able to identify other people who are dealing with those same stubborn spirits and position myself to be used by God to bless them.

Two of the most vital components to deliverance are the ability to confront ourselves and the act of forgiveness.

Your identity as a Christian has much to do with how you deal with offenses and forgiveness. Forgiveness is one way in which God imparts and conveys His nature. Forgiveness is the essence of the nature and spirit of God. So when conflicts occur, we must determine to work them out and forgive our adversaries, because that is how we grow in God.

Forgiveness is one way in which God imparts His nature.

Some people make up their minds not to work out misunderstandings and transgressions; instead, they say, "I'm just going to turn it over to the Lord."

These people are not following God's commands or His instructions for deliverance. Because they maintain their irate disposition, their health gradually succumbs to the grudge from which they refuse to be delivered.

When you refuse to follow the plan that God has established, you begin to backslide—you blame everyone else for your problems and spread the negative aura of your bad mood.

Many of the flaws that you now see in others are nothing new. In most cases, these individuals have long been as they are, but now you notice their apparent flaws because you have allowed yourself to stoop to their level.

It's not a newer revelation that you are receiving about others; rather, you are receiving a revelation about yourself.

The healing process almost always hurts, but as your wounds heal, you grow stronger and better.

When no one is in the house to pray for you or to help you to work your way to your next miracle, you must take the initiative to invoke your own deliverance.

Deliverance comes when you decide to be set free.

Deliverance comes when you decide to be set free. If you don't make that decision, you will remain bound. At some point, you must stop and say to yourself, "Enough is enough....This is the end of this....Now is the time for me to be set free!"

I found out that many people are dying for their right to hold on to the anger they harbor for a wound they received. They want to own the right to be upset. They see the car coming toward them, but because they have the right-of-way, they refuse to stop—even though their precious little ones are riding in the backseat of the car!

You could be holding on to something that you have the right to hold on to, but in the process, it's killing you on the inside.

You have the right to be upset, angry, and mad—you're right because you were wronged, but the person who wronged you is going on with his or her life, while yours has taken an abrupt halt.

Wait Patiently and Quietly for Deliverance

Jesus cast out demons and delivered people in three different postures: 1) *"immediately"* (see, for example, Matthew

8:3; 14:31 and Mark 1:31; 1:42), 2) *"that same hour"* (Matthew 8:13) or *"that very hour"* (Matthew 15:28; 17:18), and 3) *"not many days from now"* (Acts 1:5).

Many people will be set free immediately; some will have to travail with intercessors at the altar, and others will experience deliverance over a period of several years.

In fact, these people will grow into their deliverance, becoming individuals with an extraordinary knowledge of revelation and wisdom regarding demonic forces.

Silence often damages Satan's plans.

When you are under attack, the worst thing you can do is to keep talking, because this foils your strategy.

There is always *"a time to keep silence, and a time to speak"* (Ecclesiastes 3:7), and it is your responsibility to discern the times to preserve your spiritual health and well-being.

You will find that in many instances, silence will enable the greatest damage to the enemy's plans, for the spirit that is out to destroy you wants you to talk yourself into a spiritual grave. The more you talk, the more leeway Satan has to trip you up with your own words.

The more you hold your peace, the more the power of God arises within you to show you how to win the battle.

In our anger, we often spew things from our mouth and do more harm than good.

That is why, in the midst of the Israelites' complaints, Moses commanded them to hold their peace; God would fight the battle (see Exodus 14:14).

Being quiet takes practice and requires spiritual schooling, as 1 Thessalonians 4:11 says: *"ye study to be quiet, and to do your own business, and to work with your own hands"* (KJV).

There is a campaign going on in glory on behalf of your imminent victory. That is why being quiet is so difficult that the Bible says it requires training—a course in Silence 101 as a requirement to reaching your next level.

Although this is the type of attack that we will all encounter at some point, it is also one that we all have the power to overcome—with wisdom. *Wisdom* is the ability to execute properly the knowledge you already have.

How spiritual or spirited are you? "Spirited" individuals are those who are easily knocked out of the race because they make decisions based on their emotions.

When the music stops and the song has ended, the most important question is whether you know Jesus. Does He live in your heart? Can you navigate your way through life, even when there is no song?

Without a musician directing the band or dabbling with the synthesizer to let you know when something evil is about to take place, can you still discern the times?

A spiritual individual can hear God's voice even when the music stops.

This ability is what separates a "spiritual" individual from one who is simply "spirited." When the music stops playing, a spiritual individual can still hear the voice of God.

When you have conversations with people, you must be able to discern when their metaphorical horns (indicative of evil inclinations) are about to grow.

I can usually tell when an individual's conversation is about to go too far, and when I make this determination, I immediately say to him or her, "That wasn't right."

Without the ability to listen with discernment, you will get drawn in; only when it's too late will you find out that things were really not as they seemed.

You will begin to murmur regrets: "I was under an attack and I didn't even know it. I was speaking in tongues, fellowshipping with God but God never told me!"

That, of course, is a lie. God *did* tell you, but because your focus had shifted to something that was much more appealing to your flesh, you refused to listen to what God had to say.

Consequently, what you are now receiving is causing you to lose what you had. You have lost your sensitivity, your insight, and your ability to reason.

The same spirit caused an entire nation to rise up against one man: Jesus. What could a loving Savior have possibly done to incite an entire nation to rise up in outrage and kill Him?

It wasn't because He had tax problems; He paid his taxes faithfully and punctually. Instead, it was for His good deeds that He was killed—healing the sick, raising the dead, feeding the hungry on the Sabbath day, comforting a woman caught in the act of adultery, raising Lazarus from the dead, and so forth.

It was because of Jesus' good deeds that many of the people rose up against Him.

That spirit of excellence, good character, godly essence, and charismatic personality is always found in pacesetters.

What you must understand about yourself is that there are things happening in your life that do not yet have corresponding explanatory entries in the encyclopedia of life.

Why? Because you are a pacesetter, and after you have completely overcome whatever is trying to overtake you, your name and crisis are going to show up in the encyclopedia of life. You will be the one to whom others look for answers.

I know that I am called to fulfill some things that other people are not equipped to carry out. This is why I do not have to frequently go through the ritual of casting out demons.

Remaining in bondage results from a personal choice.

Instead, the Word that the Lord gives is so powerful that as I am preaching, the masses are delivered simply by hearing the Word of God as they are sitting in their seats.

Remaining in bondage comes as the result of a personal choice. The reason that pastors endure extreme hardships is often that while they are looking at the present, the devil has his eyes on the future; he will make any and every attempt to squeeze the life out of the future before it comes to pass.

Satan knows that after pastors emerge from a trial or tribulation, their example will provide answers to others regarding their own life crises.

Therefore, your job is to pray for your leaders and to avoid gossip at all costs.

In the next chapter, we will discuss how proper authority should be restored after victims of authority abuse have been delivered.

Pray that your leaders will emerge from their trials with victory and that complete healing will take place.

Prayer: *I pray in the name of Jesus for your complete freedom today from every controlling and forceful spirit that may have wrapped itself around your finances, family, marriage, relationships, health, or any other area of your life. I release you into the abundance of God's grace and pray that you will prosper and be in health, even as your soul shall prosper. I release the prosperity of your soul so that it will be manifest in your daily life. May you be set free by the power of God! In Jesus' name, amen.*

11

Restoration of Proper Authority

So I will restore to you the years that the swarming locust has eaten, the crawling locust, the consuming locust, and the chewing locust....You shall eat in plenty and be satisfied, and praise the name of the Lord your God, who has dealt wondrously with you; and My people shall never be put to shame.

Joel 2:25–26

Going down to a Samaritan city, Philip proclaimed the message of the Messiah. When the people heard what he had to say and saw the miracles, the clear signs of God's action, they hung on his every word.

Many who could neither stand nor walk were healed that day. The evil spirits protested loudly as they were sent on their way. And what joy in the city!

Previous to Philip's arrival, a certain Simon had practiced magic in the city, posing as a famous man and dazzling all the Samaritans with his wizardry He had them all, from little children to old men, eating out of his hand. They all thought he had supernatural powers, and called him "the Great Wizard." He had been around a long time, and everyone was more or less in awe of him.

But when Philip came to town announcing the news of God's kingdom and proclaiming the name of Jesus Christ, they forgot Simon and were baptized, becoming believers right and left. Even Simon himself believed and was baptized. From that moment he was like Philip's shadow, so fascinated with all the God–signs and miracles that he wouldn't leave Philip's side.

When the apostles in Jerusalem received the report that Samaria had accepted God's Message, they sent Peter and John down to pray for them to receive the Holy Spirit. Up to this point they had only been baptized in the name of the Master Jesus; the Holy Spirit hadn't yet fallen on them. Then the apostles laid their hands on them and they did receive the Holy Spirit.

When Simon saw that the apostles by merely laying on hands, conferred the Spirit, he pulled out his money, excited, and said, "Sell me your secret! Show me how you did that! How much you want? Name your price!"

Peter said, "To hell with your money! And you along with it! Why, that's unthinkable – trying to buy God's gift! You'll never be part of what God is doing by striking bargains and offering bribes. Change your ways – and now! Ask the Master to forgive you for trying to use God to make money. I can see this is an old habit with you; you reek with money–lust."

"Oh!" said Simon, "pray for me! Pray to the Master that nothing like that will ever happen to me!"

(Acts 8:9–24 MESSAGE)

Most often, this text is used as a lesson against greed or to teach the importance of pure motives. And no wonder! Simon was one of the "best" authority abusers you've ever heard of.

For years he held an entire town under his thumb. He had convinced all the residents that he was the servant of some god; maybe he was even a god himself.

Even when he had been converted and the abused townspeople were freed from his influence, he couldn't help seeing the Holy Spirit's power as means of gaining influence.

> The Spirit of God can free anyone—abused or abuser.

What I love most about this story, though, is that Simon changed. Not only does the account tell us that people can be freed from abuse by accepting Jesus; seemingly incorrigible authority abusers can change, too.

At least, that's how I read it. By the end of the story, Simon seems genuinely repentant, and I can't find any place in the Bible where God rejects true repentance.

Since the Bible doesn't say otherwise, I have to assume that, following his strong lesson in humility, Simon learned to truly love the people around him. And since, as Romans 13:10 says, *"Love does no harm to a neighbor; therefore love is the fulfillment of the law,"* I believe Simon was freed from being an authority abuser.

The weight of Scripture teaches that the Spirit of God can free anyone—abused or abuser—and restore that person to a life of wholeness and blessing.

God is the only One who can do this. He is the only One capable of restoring what the devil has killed or destroyed, and He does so with great abundance.

Die to worry, doubt, and carnality—then watch God come and restore life more abundantly.

> *Yet death held sway from Adam to Moses [the Lawgiver], even over those who did not themselves transgress [a positive command] as Adam did. Adam was a type (prefigure) of the One Who was to come [in reverse, the former destructive, the Latter saving]. But God's free gift is not at all to be compared to the trespass [His grace is out of all proportion to the fall of man]. For if many died through one man's falling away (his lapse, his offense), much more profusely did God's grace and the free gift [that comes] through the undeserved favor of the one Man Jesus Christ abound and overflow to and for [the benefit of] many. Nor is the free gift at all to be compared to the effect of that one [man's] sin. For the sentence [following the trespass] of one [man] brought condemnation, whereas the free gift [following] many transgressions brings justification (an act of righteousness). For if because of one man's trespass (lapse, offense) death reigned through that one, much more surely will those who receive [God's] overflowing grace (unmerited favor) and the free gift of righteousness [putting them into right standing with Himself] reign as kings in life through the one Man Jesus Christ (the Messiah, the Anointed One).* (Romans 5:14–17 AMP)

Verse 15 says,

> *But God's free gift is not at all to be compared to the trespass....For if many died through one man's falling away..., much more profusely did God's grace and the free gift [that comes] through the undeserved favor of the one Man Jesus Christ abound and overflow to and for [the benefit of] many.* (AMP)

Though worded differently, this verse is a repeat of John 10:10. God says, in effect, "Okay, you sinned, and the penalty is death. The thief came to you; he stole from you and robbed you, but I'm going to give you a free gift, and the free gift is life."

God says, "I'm going to resurrect you out of a mind-set that has kept you in bondage. I'm going to set you free—not in your own righteousness, but in the righteousness of God."

> *Nor is the free gift at all to be compared to the effect of that one [man's] sin. For the sentence [following the trespass] of one [man] brought condemnation, whereas the free gift [following] many transgressions brings justification.*
> (Romans 5:16 AMP)

One person sinned and caused sin to fall on everyone, but the God of "much more" consoles and restores us by promising, "I'll forgive you." His grace is powerful enough and He will forgive you.

Grace is God's commitment to erase your sins and execute His rescue mission to free you from the enemy's elaborate snares.

He alone, then, justifies you by faith—forgives you, cleans you up, and shreds the evidence of your past transgressions.

That is why Romans 8:1 declares, *"Therefore, [there is] now no condemnation (no adjudging guilty of wrong) for those who are in Christ Jesus"* (AMP).

Returning to Romans 5:17 (AMP),

> *For if because of one man's trespass (lapse, offense) death reigned through that one, much more surely will those who receive [God's] overflowing grace (unmerited favor) and the free gift of righteousness [putting them into right standing with Himself] reign as kings in life through the one Man Jesus Christ (the Messiah, the Anointed One).*

The Bible actually says that the point of receiving the gift of righteousness is where one's release of the penalty of sin is found.

> The power of Jesus makes you worthy to be blessed.

The vision for your life will never come to full fruition as long as you subscribe to guilt and condemnation. It is the cleansing power of Jesus Christ that makes you feel worthy enough to be blessed.

Often we tell people that they're not worthy enough to be blessed, fueling the rejection that might already be festering inside their emotional closet. Instead, we sometimes need to tell individuals they're doing a good job so their confidence level can rise to a standard of assurance of themselves in God.

I speak from experience, for I suffered rejection as a child. I had to go through a period of growth before I learned how to encourage myself, walk in the Spirit of God, and develop a true relationship with Him for myself. Other Christians play an important part in this growth process.

> *This I say then, walk in the Spirit, and ye shall not fulfil the lust of the flesh.* (Galatians 5:16 KJV)

Everything that the devil has twisted and taken in your life, you have the power and authority to demand he put back. Every lamp he's overturned in your tidy room of righteousness and peace, he has to set aright again.

Although you've made some mistakes in your life, if you continue to seek God and praise Him, He will restore the devastation that canker worms have inflicted on your mind and in your life.

> *The threshing floors shall be full of wheat, and the vats shall overflow with new wine and oil. So I will restore to you the years that the swarming locust has eaten, the crawling locust, the consuming locust, and the chewing locust, My great army which I sent among you. You shall eat in plenty and be satisfied, and praise the name of the* LORD *your God, who has dealt wondrously with you; and My people shall never be put to shame.* (Joel 2:24–26)

The Lord declares that you are the righteousness of God, bought with a price. Though you're warring with two nations, who you really are will eventually come forth and you'll find that person to be nothing like what the devil tried to convince you was inside.

Too many times we believe the voice of Lucifer instead of the divine destiny God has spoken and ordained for our lives.

> *God is not a man, that He should lie, nor a son of man, that He should repent. Has He said, and will He not do? Or has He spoken, and will He not make it good?*
> (Numbers 23:19)

God has already told the principalities that you are anointed; He is not intimidated by what intimidates many others, such as your past or your present situation.

He knew your ending before your beginning and is not swayed when it appears to others that you're not going to make it.

> How can we say we love God and not show His forgiveness to others?

Some of us are still living off prayers our mothers or fathers prayed over us when we were children. God has forgiven us all of some great trespasses and has restored what the enemy said was destroyed forever.

If God can forgive us of the offensive acts we've committed, then we in turn should learn to forgive others of their trespasses against us.

How can we say we love God and not exercise His gift of forgiveness? You, who were dead in trespasses and sin, the thief came and destroyed; but God came and brought you back to life. God is using your testimony to show the world His grace, His goodness, and His power.

You're not going to enjoy the benefits of a solid relationship with God by continuing to worry about yesterday's experiences and being too afraid to face tomorrow.

Thank God for today! He did not begin loving you when you turned from sin and began seeking Him; rather, He loved you while you were yet in your sinful "yesterday."

He loved you in spite of you. The love of God is not something we deserve. It is a gift, and even when you've blown it, He still loves you and shows up where you are to pull you out of the quagmire of confusion and place your feet upon a solid foundation of stability.

Jesus said, *"If you abide in My word, you are My disciples indeed. And you shall know the truth, and the truth shall make you free"* (John 8:31–32).

With this book, I am doing my best to help you see the truth about authority abuse. The spirit of Jezebel has been at work in the world for so long that hardly anyone has been immune to its influence.

Fathers, mothers, pastors, teachers, youth leaders, husbands, wives—people all around us are clawing desperately for control and depending on the manipulation of people for their security instead of on Christ.

I hope that, by the grace of God, this book has enabled you to see any abuse that might be lurking in your life.

Simply recognizing that it is there and that it is a perversion of God's plan is a huge step.

As we've discussed, abusive leaders usually try to make their victims feel personally at fault for the abuse instead of admitting that it is their sin that has gone haywire.

If you can see abuse for what it is, you have taken a major step toward freedom—even if you are the abuser.

Ask God to show you the true state of your heart.

Let me strongly urge you: if you have the slightest feeling that you may be trapped in abusive behavior patterns, seek God! Ask Him to show you the true state of your heart.

Remember, He takes this seriously, but He will never reject a repentant heart. The apostle Paul was a murderer who hated God and openly oppressed His people.

Yet when he acknowledged he was wrong and surrendered to God, he was restored. Not only that, but God also used Paul as one of the most effective servants the kingdom has ever known.

If You Have Been an Abuser

If you've been an abuser, the first thing you have to do is accept responsibility. I know many abusers are trying to salvage their lives from the abuse someone has inflicted on them, but that doesn't excuse you.

If you want to find the wholeness God has for you, you must face your sin without trying to make it seem any less than it really is; then, you need to take it to God.

When you ask His forgiveness, you will have to repent. That's an old-school word for "change your mind" or "turn around and go the other way." It is a lot like breaking an addiction to drugs.

I know this is an apt analogy because the Lord delivered me from a cocaine habit that, at its worst, cost me about five hundred dollars a day.

When I first quit, I did it cold turkey. This didn't last, because all I had done was dredge up all my willpower to suppress my ever-present need for the next fix.

I had to quit a second time through a careful detoxification program. Through this program, I adopted a life of discipline—I stopped spending time in places where I could buy cocaine if I wanted it, I worked on developing good habits to fill the time I used to spend stoned, and I began "medicating" myself daily with the Word of God and prayer.

Obviously, a daily dose of time with God brought the most powerful change in my life. *"The Lord...inclined to me, and heard my cry. He also brought me up out of a horrible pit, out of the miry clay, and set my feet upon a rock, and established my steps"* (Psalm 40:1–2).

But I had to honor the work He was doing by disciplining myself to break old habits.

Medicate yourself with daily Bible study and prayer.

You must apply the same principles to the "addiction" of authority abuse. Medicate yourself every day with time in prayer and Bible study.

Get God's truth into your bloodstream; it will change you. And develop a practice of using less authority than you actually have.

Yes, that's what I said—voluntarily reduce your own authority. The extra humility and discipline will make room for God to work in your heart.

You see, I know that having authority can be kind of fun. If I'm in my office and feeling pretty good about myself, I could tell you, "Hey, watch this."

Then I'd bark at one of my assistants, "Hey you! Grab me that paper off the table!"

You know what? He'd do it with a smile, because that's the kind of authority I have in my office. I don't have to get up for anything I don't want to, but I make a habit of doing my own fetching and carrying whenever I can.

You'll never lose by doing a little work instead of flexing your authority.

Finally, as you engage in this life of discipline, get yourself under someone else's authority. Remember what the centurion said to Jesus—that authority must be delegated from above? If you don't have someone over you to whom you can be accountable, you're not a safe person to have in leadership.

You simply can't ask people to do what you are unwilling to do. Before Jesus asked us to give Him our lives, He sacrificed His own life for us. Before you can ask anyone to submit to you, your own will must be submitted to a God-ordained authority.

I know this all sounds pretty simple. I can almost hear someone asking, "So that's all he has to do? An abusive leader can just repent, submit himself, and then discipline his life? That's it?"

My answer is, "Yes."

Natural consequences aside (if he broke the law, then that will have to be dealt with), that's all. That's all Jesus ever asks from us. All He wants is all of us.

When we reject our sin, come to Him, and truly make Him master of ourselves, there is nothing left to give. That's when grace begins to work.

I pray that no one who reads this book will put it down without asking God, "What about me? What kind of steward have I been with the authority You've given me?"

And whatever the answer, I pray it will drive you to lean on Him more than ever before.

If You Have Been a Victim

If you have been a victim, God wants to restore proper authority in your life. I understand that if you are just recognizing how abusive an authority over you has been, restoring authority might not sound like good news.

Let me explain how you can start down the path to restoration, though. If you'll come along, I believe that your heart will be healed and ready for whatever God wants to do in your life by the time you reach the end.

Step One: Forgiveness

The first thing you have to do is find the high ground of forgiveness. Climb up out of the muddy swamp of grudge-holding and rest on the higher plain of forgiveness, where the wind of the Holy Spirit can waft away the stench that clings to you.

As I've mentioned before, I grew up with an overbearing father who was abusive whenever he wasn't absent. He didn't provide for our family, and he blamed us for most of his problems.

My pastor was much like my father. When I was twelve, I met another form of abuse: a thirty-year-old woman, one of my mother's friends, sexually molested me while I was at her house.

This abuse left such a painful scar on my heart that, for years, I only had to close my eyes to be able to see every detail of the room in which it occurred. I remember the music that was playing, and hearing that song still twists my stomach in knots. I can give you the exact street, house, and apartment number where she lived.

Unless you forgive an abuser, you will never put abuse behind you.

But I don't have to relive the pain from those situations anymore. It did not make me a permanently abusive father, nor have I ever had the slightest desire to molest a child.

I remember those things on purpose now because they are a testimony to what God can do in a broken life. These experiences helped make me a compassionate leader and remind me of why Jesus said, *"It would be better for him if a millstone were hung around his neck, and he were thrown into the sea, than that he should offend one of these little ones"* (Luke 17:2).

Now, about forgiveness: the Bible's teaching about forgiveness is pretty incredible. Jesus said, *"For if you forgive men their trespasses, your heavenly Father will also forgive you. But if you do not forgive men their trespasses, neither will your Father forgive your trespasses"* (Matthew 6:14–15).

He also told a parable about a servant who was forgiven of a huge debt (like the sin-debt we owe to God) but refused to forgive his neighbor of a few-dollars' debt.

Jesus said that, as a result, the unforgiving man was called to account for his own debt even though he and his family were ruined forever.

God demands that we forgive. I've found a reason to forgive that may appeal even more to an outraged victim, though. After all, it's hard to accept that we should forgive an abuser just because "God said so."

That should be a good enough reason for anyone, but I've personally experienced emotions that say otherwise! So, try this on for size: *Unless you forgive the abuser, you will never be able to put the abuse behind you.*

It's true: as long as you hold the abuser responsible for his actions, your sense of justice will keep the abuse active in your mind as unfinished business.

You see, the enemy does his best to trap us coming and going, and our fallen nature cooperates far too easily!

People stop drinking but start smoking. They stop smoking but start overeating. They swear off drinking coffee but start drinking soda. They break free from an abusive situation but become trapped in bitterness.

Only when you pardon the abuser—a pardon he doesn't deserve—will you be able to lay the issue to rest. *"Beloved, do not avenge yourselves, but rather give place to wrath; for it is written, 'Vengeance is Mine, I will repay,' says the Lord"* (Romans 12:19).

It takes a lot of trust, but you have to believe that God will take care of what needs to be done. Once you get a grasp on this, it is very liberating. You can simply hand the abuser over to God and say, "Take care of this guy for me, okay?"

Do not join the perfect church; you will ruin it!

Then you can forget about it, because God is a completely righteous judge, and He will do what is best.

The Bible says that if you don't forgive, you won't be forgiven. Not only that, but you won't be free from the pain of your abuse, either. So you could conceivably leave an abusive situation only to wind up in another equally abusive one.

I have seen women do this time and again. Because they left bad relationships without letting God clear their heads or heal their hearts, they went straight into the arms of other abusive men.

I have seen people do the same with churches, too. Sometimes a wounded person will go to a perfectly healthy church and take his wounds with him.

Because of the bitterness inside, he flails around, trying to keep himself "safe," but he winds up hurting innocent people around him.

I think this is why so many pastors say, "If you find the perfect church, don't join it—you'll ruin it!"

Sometimes we must deal with the mess inside our hearts before we can fix whatever mess goes on outside.

Don't misunderstand what it means to forgive. You cannot say "it's okay" when someone abuses you. It's not okay. What he did was wrong, no matter what good God wants to bring out of it. It was sin, and nothing you say or do can change that.

You didn't cause him to sin, and his own circumstances cannot justify his actions. Sin is sin. Abuse is always abuse. You are releasing him from your personal judgment, but he still has to face God's judgment.

C. S. Lewis gave a splendid description of this mind-set in his book, *Mere Christianity*:

> "For a long time I used to think this a silly, straw-splitting distinction: how could you hate what a man did and not hate the man? But years later it occurred to me that there was one man to whom I had been doing this all my life—namely myself. However much I might dislike my own cowardice or conceit or greed, I went on loving myself. There had never been the slightest difficulty about it. In fact the very reason why I hated the things was that I loved the man. Just because I loved myself, I was sorry to find that I was the sort of man who did those things. Consequently, Christianity does not want us to reduce by one atom the hatred we feel for cruelty and treachery. We ought to hate them. Not one word of what we have said about them needs to be unsaid. But it does want us to hate them in the same way in which we hate things in

> ourselves: being sorry that the man should have done such things, and hoping, if it is anyway possible, that somehow, sometime, somewhere he can be cured and made human again."[1]

Step Two: Adjusting Your Life

"What?" I can hear someone asking. "My life has been turned inside out by an abusive leader. I don't want to *adjust!* I want to get back to normal!"

I can understand that; but if you were the strong, insightful person that God designed you to be, how were you trapped by an authority abuser in the first place? Don't you believe God wants you to be able to see what's wrong in a situation like that and avoid it altogether?

If that's true, why would you want to go back to what you used to call "normal"?

Yes, you need to be free from bitterness and pain. But should you refuse to learn anything or to grow?

No. God wants to build you into a person you never knew you could be. He wants to show you your true self. He wants you to flourish under godly authority.

It may sound strange at first, but the process for building your new life is the same as for a former abuser. You must adopt a life of discipline so that you take in God's truth and grace on a daily basis.

Mull over what the Word says about you:

> *You are not your own....For you were bought at a price; therefore glorify God in your body and in your spirit, which are God's.* (1 Corinthians 6:19–20)

> *Are not five sparrows sold for two copper coins? And not one of them is forgotten before God. But the very hairs of your head are all numbered. Do not fear therefore; you are of more value than many sparrows.* (Luke 12:6–7)

> *Who shall separate us from the love of Christ? Shall tribulation, or distress, or persecution, or famine, or nakedness, or peril, or sword?....In all these things we are more than conquerors through Him who loved us. For I am persuaded that neither death nor life, nor angels nor principalities nor powers, nor things present nor things to come, nor height nor depth, nor any other created thing, shall be able to separate us from the love of God which is in Christ Jesus our Lord.* (Romans 8:35–39)

Get used to making prayer a conversation with God. Don't be afraid to tell Him, "God, I'm asking for Your help because I need it."

You can't create the new you, and you can't force yourself to become stronger and wiser.

But you can ask God for help with it. God promised, *"If any of you lacks wisdom, let him ask of God, who gives to all liberally and without reproach, and it will be given to him"* (James 1:5).

Then He cautioned, *"But let him ask in faith, with no doubting, for he who doubts is like a wave of the sea driven and tossed by the wind"* (v. 6).

Ask God and believe that He will supply the wisdom.

Be patient with yourself. You will make mistakes, so don't assume God didn't give you wisdom when you asked or that He never sent His grace to be your strength.

Building a life is a process. Remember, though, you have a wonderful promise in His Word: *"He who has begun a good work in you will complete it until the day of Jesus Christ"* (Philippians 1:6).

Step Three: Submitting to Godly Authority

As God began to heal the wounds I received at the hands of abusive leaders, I wasn't looking for an authority to submit to.

I guess I must have known in the back of my mind that I would need some kind of spiritual leadership or accountability some day, but I was simply focused on what God put right in front of me.

> Believers must be part of a healthy church.

Imagine my surprise, then, when God put in front of me authority figures I could trust and respect!

I don't think I'm in a place where I can tell you to run out and start hunting for someone to submit to. I do know God will want to set you under an authority who will bless and nurture the work He is doing in you, though, and He will provide such a person in His time.

I also know that all believers need to be a part of a healthy, well-balanced church, and I do think you should make finding one a priority.

Don't expect to find a perfect church; just look for one that houses God's presence and sincerely seeks to apply His truth to its community.

Finding the right church may not be a quick process, but make sure you're not holding each place up to your own standards of what a church should be.

Instead, ask God whether what He is doing in you and what He is doing in that church makes the two of you a match.

When you find the church where you belong, you will have to submit yourself to the leadership. You don't have to throw yourself on the floor before your pastor and grovel. As you spend time in the church, however, he should be able to get to know you, get a feel for who you are, and have some input in your life.

You will have to trust again; but when your ultimate trust is in the Lord, you'll have the courage to give it a shot.

I believe that, eventually, you will *"be like a tree planted by the rivers of water, that brings forth its fruit in its season, whose leaf also shall not wither; and whatever* [you do] *shall prosper"* (Psalm 1:3).

Your pastor (or other leader) will be like a skilled gardener, pruning your branches and watering the soil you're rooted in. By God's grace, authority will be at work once again.

Endnote

[1]C. S. Lewis, *Mere Christianity* (San Francisco: HarperCollins, 2001), 117–118.

Discussion Questions and Journal

Reflect on what the Lord taught you in each chapter of this book, using these questions to guide your study. You may also choose to discuss your responses in a group setting. Think about what changes you will need to make as a result of God's word to you.

After each set of discussion questions, space is provided for you to record your reflections and thoughts for future reference and personal growth.

Chapter One

Like all evil, authority abuse is a perversion of something God intended to beautiful.

1. What is one word to describe this kind of evil?

____

2. God takes authority abuse very seriously. What was the real punishment Jesus described for the wicked foreman in Matthew 24:44–55?

____

____

____

____

____

____

Journal

____

____

____

____

____

____

____

____

____

Chapter Two

True authority is from above.

1. Who first set up the order of authority?

___

2. What is authority for?

___

3. Explain in your own words why authority is necessary in a world of free will.

___

___

___

___

Journal

___

___

___

___

___

___

___

___

___

___

Chapter Three

Authority can be intoxicating.

1. What kinds of leaders are most at risk of being overcome by it?

____

____

____

2. In your own words, give two reasons that people abuse their authority.

1) ____________________________________

____

2) ____________________________________

____

Journal

____

____

____

____

____

____

____

____

____

Chapter Four

1. Give a simple definition of authority abuse:

____

____

2. List five ways to recognize authority abuse:

1) ______________________________

2) ______________________________

3) ______________________________

4) ______________________________

5) ______________________________

3. Now, in your own words, explain your answers to the previous question.

____

____

____

____

Journal

____

____

____

____

____

____

Chapter Five

A biblical view of finances will teach you to eat your bread and sow your seed.

1. What is your "bread"?

2. What is your "seed"?

3. Does God promise to make you wealthy? Explain your response.

Journal

Chapter Six

1. Who has the first responsibility to keep an abusive leader out of the home?

2. What is the simplest way to do this?

3. Define in your own words what it means for a husband and wife to be "one flesh."

Journal

Chapter Seven

1. Does the Bible support the idea that a man should be "king" of his house?

2. Why does a husband have authority over his wife?

3. Is it ever right in God's sight to deprive your spouse of what he or she genuinely needs? Why or why not?

Journal

Chapter Eight

1. Is godly authority democratic? Why or why not?

2. Think about a situation in which you had trouble submitting to the authority over you. If you didn't deal with this problem, would it affect your ability to lead other people in a godly way? Why or why not?

Journal

Chapter Nine

1. What does it mean to "medicate" yourself with God's Word and prayer?

___

2. What about forgiveness is hardest for you? What can you do to open your heart and allow God to love through you?

___

___

___

___

3. Explain how you can seek a life of discipline in order to discover the person God wants you to be. How can you personally apply this to your schedule?

___

___

___

___

Journal

___

___

___

___

___

___

___

Chapter Ten

1. List the similarities between authority abusers and python snakes. Why is a python snake an apt analogy for the spirit of authority abuse?

2. Why is it important to spend time in private conversation and communion with God? What will He reveal to you?

3. What is the difference between being "spiritual" and being "spirited"? Evaluate yourself in terms of these words and think about how you can be more as you should be.

Journal

Chapter Eleven

1. What is the most compelling reason for us as Christians to forgive others?

____

2. List the three primary steps an authority abuser must follow to put a stop to this sinful behavior and make restitution with those he or she has wronged.

1)____

2)____

3)____

3. List the three steps a victim of authority abuse must take to receive healing.

1)____

2)____

3)____

Journal

____

____

____

____

____

____

____

About the Author

G. G. Bloomer

Bishop George G. Bloomer is a native of Brooklyn, New York. Now residing in Durham, North Carolina, with his wife and two daughters, he is the founder and senior pastor of Bethel Life Family Worship Center.

The product of humble beginnings, he has climbed the ladder of success and now uses those learning experiences as priceless tools for empowering others to excel beyond the boundaries of physical limitations.

In June of 1996, Bloomer fashioned a thirty-day tent revival in the heart of downtown Durham, North Carolina. Subsequent to its closing, Bethel Family Worship Center was birthed in a small office building with approximately twenty members.

With its swift growth soon came the need for expansion. The expansion of the ministry led to the purchase of what today houses a multicultural and diverse congregation.

Today, Bloomer not only pastors, but he can be heard speaking weekly throughout the country and abroad to Christian and secular society on various topics of interest.

Bishop Bloomer holds a degree of Doctor of Religious Arts in Christian Psychology and conducts many seminars dealing with relationships, finances, stress management, and spiritual warfare.

He has appeared on several television programs and radio talk shows, including CNN's *Faces of Faith,* Trinity Broadcasting Network, and *The 700 Club.*

Bloomer's national broadcast, *Spiritual Authority,* can be seen each Sunday morning and viewed live online on Tuesdays and Sundays. He continues to travel extensively throughout the nation, delivering a message to liberate and impact the lives of thousands for Christ.

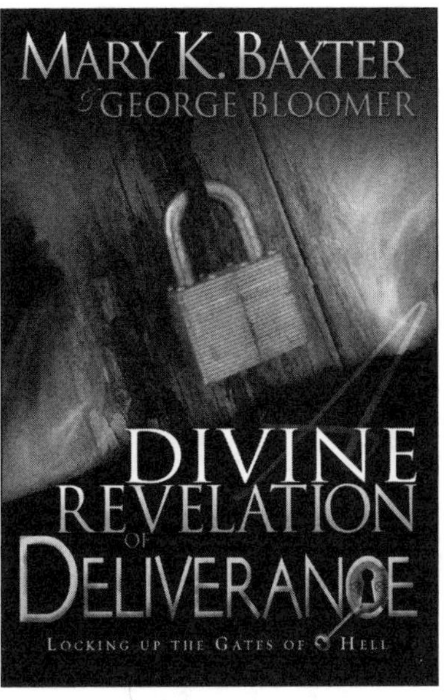

A Divine Revelation of Deliverance

Mary K. Baxter
with George G. Bloomer

Many Christians live with frustration and defeat. They wonder why they can't overcome sins and temptations, even though they pray and try to be strong. Yet God loves us and wants to set us free. Through Christ, He gives us victory over the enemy and the power to deliver others who are pawns of Satan's destructive plans. Mary K. Baxter exposes Satan's schemes and provides much-needed hope for the suffering and oppressed. Receive a divine revelation of your deliverance in Christ!

ISBN: 978-0-88368-754-3 • Trade • 224 pages

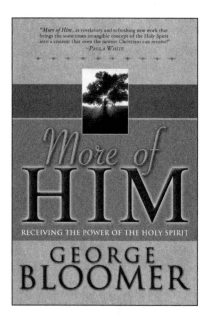

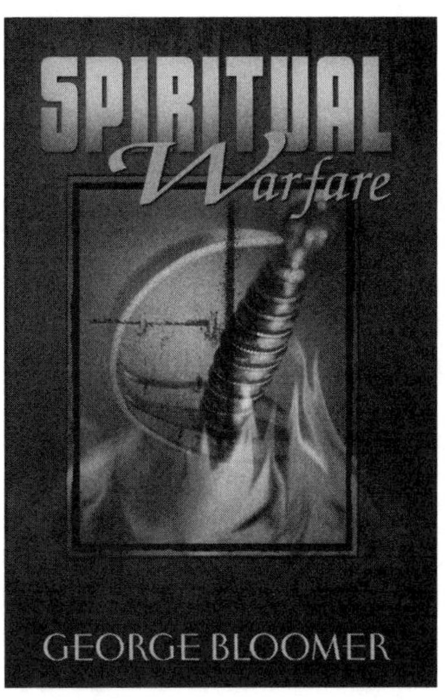

Spiritual Warfare

George G. Bloomer

Guilt? Shame? Fear? Mental anguish? Intimidation? Are spiritual attacks holding you back? Fellow warrior George Bloomer shows how to effectively silence Satan's roar by using God's authority. Learn how to identify Satan's strategies and block his attacks, experience victory over fear and bondage, and receive God's promises for your every need. Equip yourself with biblical principles of spiritual warfare and reap the rewards of a joyous life!

ISBN: 978-0-88368-683-6 • Trade • 208 pages

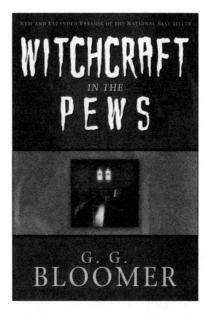